*fearless
future*

fearless future

A Map Through an Uncertain Present

Louise Platt Hauck

www.louisehauck.com

Lamplight Publishing Company
511 6th Avenue, Ste. 234
New York, NY 10011

www.louisehauck.com

ISBN 0-9769205-0-6

Publisher's Cataloging-in-Publication Data
(Prepared by The Donohue Group, Inc.)

Hauck, Louise Platt.
　　Fearless future : a map through an uncertain present /
Louise Platt Hauck.
　　　　p. ; cm.
　　ISBN: 0-9769205-0-6
　　1. Hauck, Louise Platt.　2. Extrasensory
perception.　3. Spiritual life.　4. Reincarnation.
5. Consciousness.　6. Space and time. I. Title.
BF1321 .H38　　2005
133.8

Printed in the United States of America

Contents

Acknowledgements

Time is an illusion, yet timing is everything. Michael Butler returned from National Guard duty in Iraq, just as I was relocating from London to Connecticut. We met years ago in an Internet discussion group on spirituality when a 1200 baud modem was something to shout about. Combine skill in editing military intelligence reports and a focused intention to help make *Fearless Future* a "definitive piece" and you have one appreciative author.

Joanne Pavia forever arrives—eleventh hour—to contribute to my project du jour. Her keen eyes have are famous for spotting errors in leather bound books. Lynn Shuler joined in and matched her editing skill. Pat Barrentine is another ongoing eleventh-hour angel, always there to contribute a good eye and a focus that will have helped to save this planet.

John Hughes anchors me and extends truly unconditional love from London. Annie Osburn bestowed remarkable editing and publicist skills, while Kathy Routt kept Illuminations humming when book duty called. Glenn Levy, Jaene Leonard, Cindy Mayfield, Ann Hoeffel, Tracy Ferron, Nancy Slakoff, Lisbet Ahrenkilde—and my beloved apprentices—forever cheer me onward. Pat and Ted Nelson, Maryann and Tom Bankman, Joy and Howard Cohen—all made Connecticut a safe and wonderful haven for me. The love and support of Greg Ryan made this book a reality. Dylan, my son and webmaster, continues to extend the vision of my work and never stops believing in me. My deepest and sincere thanks to you all.

Preface

"Prod! Prod! Like this!"

A salesgirl was jabbing my left arm, as she stood before me in the middle of Marks and Spencer. She persisted in a very intense manner.

"Prod! See? Prod!"

I took a step back, slowly, to avoid being the target of her torpedo-like pointy finger, while trying not to appear unappreciative of her attempt to communicate with such deliberate intention.

"I'm sorry, I don't understand . . ."

"PROD! PROD-juice! Get it? PROD-juice!"

Direct hit. Another jab delivered as she stepped towards me, as if coming closer and pushing harder would clarify our communication. We spoke the same language, yet I had no idea what this woman was trying to say.

"PROD-juice!" she repeated, this time with greater amplitude.

"Prod-juice? OH! PRO-duce! You're saying, PRO-duce!" I said, relieved, and proud of my sudden epiphany.

"Pro-duce?" the woman asked, looking puzzled.

Our conversation continued like this for a few more moments, until we finally negotiated a mutual understanding. I had simply asked where to find a head of red cabbage. My hostess for the holiday had asked me to pick one up for Christmas dinner.

Now the determined salesgirl marched down one aisle and over three, looking back over her shoulder to make sure I was following her to the produce section. The store was filled with last-minute shoppers on this Christmas Eve. Fathers searched for last-minute gifts that would probably garner as much appreciation as those grabbed up in airport gift shops as afterthoughts. Mothers stood in the checkout lines, their trolleys (baskets) filled with cranky children, nappies (diapers) and poinsettias, reduced to half-price.

I had arrived in England only a few days before, allowing time for my traditional stay with my friends in Winchester, before taking the train into London. This was a wonderful routine, developed over almost ten years of trips to this country to give presentations and meet with clients. This time I had arrived in London to make it my home.

Leaving NYC

Time was a blur after September 11, 2001, when I watched the horrible disaster unfold from my rooftop in Manhattan. The images are instantly retrievable, vivid and lasting in my mind. Dark specks that were people swelled out onto one side of the last tower to collapse. They appeared like blobs emerging from a monolithic, concrete cocoon, then fell into the billows of smoke and debris below. A ring of fire above them emblazoned a foreboding announcement of their imminent deaths, burning brighter than the neon lights of Times Square. I held my head and sobbed.

"It's okay . . . It will be okay . . ." comforted a young student from China who stood nearby.

"It's not okay!" I cried, unable to comprehend what I was seeing. The girl seemed more disturbed by my own grief than by the actuality of all that was happening before us. She continued to pat my shoulder, nervously. It seemed as though her focus on comforting me served to distract herself from the horror.

A close friend stood beside me. Jaene lived in the same building and worked as my assistant, as well as being a talented actor and playwright. From the first day we met in Manhattan, we felt a wonderful resonance with each other. She came to awaken me after the report of a plane plowing into the first tower. Together we ran to the roof. The deeply emotional experience that we witnessed that day has bonded us forever, as shared tragedies often do.

I was relieved to hear that those who jumped from such a great height to avoid death by fire and smoke would have lost consciousness before landing. However, being an "intuitive" by nature and profession, it is not unusual for me to see—and often interpret for—souls who have made the transition from their physical bodies. My work continually gives evidence of death to be the falling away of the body, *not* the demise of the soul, nor of the spirit that ignites it and propels it forward through lifetimes. It was with this understanding that I watched countless souls eject from their physical bodies in those tormenting moments.

Furthermore, I have concluded that in instances of sudden or violent deaths, the soul most often ejects from the body before impact. This is confirmed whenever I am allowed to merge with a loved one's timeless conscious and experience what they experienced at the time of their "death."

I experienced that one client's husband had ejected from his physical body where it had been seated on a bus in Jerusalem, just before the bus was blown apart by a suicide bomber. Until that soul came to the realization that he now existed beyond his physical self, he thought he was watching this whole scene on the five o'clock news! Then he came to the realization that it was actually his own body that he was viewing, laying there on the street.

Therefore, even though a continuum of consciousness maintains as the soul makes its transition from the physical to a non-physical dimension, it is unlikely that those who jumped from the Twin Towers remained in their bodies long enough to have experienced the loss of consciousness. I saw them lift out and up, a herd of souls making its way to the Light, even before their bodies fell to the ground below. I sent those souls the telepathic message to head that way with God's blessing. I also sent prayers.

Through those weeks, it amazed me that amidst the chaos and debris there was a higher and more expanded, extremely intuitive and overseeing part of my consciousness that continued to operate, unfazed by the surreal images around Manhattan. That aspect of my timeless self continued to be in tune and to thrive, even while all that was illusionary in my world was falling away.

A few days after the disaster, I consulted for Beth, a new client who was referred by Carol, her co-worker. Both employees work for a disaster agency, at that time assigned to Ground Zero. I had read Carol a month before, in Chicago. She is a long-time client from several years back who I had only "met" and consulted for by phone. She drove six hours to Chicago so that we could finally meet in person. I felt honored, to say the least.

When the Twin Towers went down, I had a vague recollection of having viewed the scene of "a tall building falling down" in several consultations, during that week in Chicago. I saw it again in a consultation that I did the night just before the disaster at the uptown New York Marriott Hotel. At the time, I interpreted the images more as time-sequence signposts for more relevant information, rather than signaling imminent disaster. "And after a building falls, you'll be . . ."

That was the context within which I relayed this information before September 11th, when I *did* happen to mention these images, as opposed to other instances when I discarded them, yielding to others scenes that *seemed* more important at the time.

Usually, when it is time to "download" collected information in consultations, I have to decide how to arrange and prioritize the information in the order of that which appears to be most relevant and significant. As my apprentices learn, most information comes in "neutral." The interpretation given to any intuited information is unavoidably filtered by the "receiver's" own repertoire of experiences. Terrorism had not been part of mine.

I asked Beth, "Did Carol hear me mention anything about a tall building falling when I read her in Chicago?" I was unable to recall whether or not I had given it emphasis.

"Yes!" she said. "She listened again to the tape and heard you saying, 'After tall building with a long antenna falls [you weren't sure what the antenna was], you will be working near water.' That's where Carol is today, working at Ground Zero. You also mentioned something about a ship. You thought that perhaps she might be going on a cruise. She eats everyday on the USS Comfort, docked at the piers near the site."

No longer could I glibly reassure clients, "I only get positive or preventative information." I do not tend to access information regarding global or political predictions, international events or the affairs of high-profile people. I view images through the timeless consciousness of my clients, able to move scenes forwards and backwards through time. I see through their eyes where their timeless selves are experiencing strategic future moments. I access this information for the purpose of exploring examples of their spiritual development in potentially happier futures. Then I contrast those future moments with challenges that exist in the present, thereby opening a corridor between the present and future. Emphasizing the positive aspects of those futures encourages clients to face down that corridor. The likelihood of the most positive future unfolding depends upon the degree to which clients awaken and integrate new learning and insights along the way.

With *this* particular client, however, I tend to preview scenes that turn out to *be* global in nature. She happens to work for an agency that deals with national emergencies. It is her job to show up at disaster sites. Disaster is in her future.

A few days after September 11th, Carol asked me to come to her hotel in Times Square for another consultation. Once again, through her future consciousness, I saw pertinent images. I said, "In this future moment, you've been pulled 'from all the bright colors.'" She reminded me that I had made a similar reference in several previous consultations, describing a time when she would find herself "around many bright colors." We had both attempted a few likely interpretations, images within the context of what was plausible at the time: A future interest in home decorating? Working with a collection of flower essence bottles?

"Geez!" I exclaimed, opening my eyes to look out her hotel window. "Here are the bright colored lights of Times Square! I admired them when I got off the elevator!" Then I proceeded with her consultation. And once again, I found myself experiencing a future moment through her timeless consciousness, where she was on assignment at yet another disaster that might follow 9/11.

I proceeded to describe the images that I viewed while "hanging out" at the future site. So disturbing were the possible interpretations of those images that the next day I felt compelled to phone an old client who still worked for the FBI. I passed the information on to her, describing what I saw in great detail in as many different ways as I could interpret. I alerted authorities that could potentially be involved and tried to release the possibilities and the images from my mind. I reaffirmed that I only seek to receive and interpret positive and preventive information that is for my clients' highest good to receive.

Unfortunately, this disturbing experience clung to me like unpleasant goo that was too sticky to shake loose. It added negative weight to other associations regarding my life in New York City. Approaching my eighth year in Manhattan, I had come to feel numbed by the cumulative effects of frenetic and noisy metropolitan life. More recently, I felt abused and worn by the constant reminders of the horrific sights, sounds and sorrow that replayed and echoed unforgettably around me.

I felt increasingly more unconscious in my daily after-work routine that focused on calculated escapes from my small living space. Cafés with no-smoking sections were havens for my reading and writing. I escaped to movies that cost more than those in any other town I had lived. I had always been an avid moviegoer. If I were Catholic, I suppose that a confession of my most grievous sin would have to be: "Forgive me father, for I have sinned. When asked to pay $9.50 for movies in Manhattan, more than once I have stood at the ticket window, removed my baseball cap, brushed down my salt-and-pepper bangs and asked for senior-priced tickets."

In New York, I lived with an ongoing bruise on my outer left thigh, caused by banging it against a pull-down desk whenever I reached around and into my tiny closet to retrieve a fax. The space was very dark, given the absence of light and the presence of so much "New York black" clothing. Every time I reached in to grab a fax from my Hewlett Packard, it seemed to mock me, spitting out faxes from where it was perched on an inaccessible wicker file box under a curtain of coats and hanging belts. I used to tell my friends, "You know you're living in a small space when your faxes get rolled up into coat sleeves."

I ate more ice cream in the two weeks following 9/11 than I had consumed in the previous ten years. Hagen Daas: Vanilla Swiss Almond and Mint Chip in a sugar cone. I took note of this somewhat addictive behavior, and watched circles darken under my eyes, accompanied by a persistent, dull headache. I normally eat wisely and have not experienced headaches since I started meditating, almost thirty years ago.

Haunting images delayed my sleep at night until, after a few prayers, I would consciously breathe into my self-healing-cleansing-relaxation visualization and drift off for at least six hours—only one or two short of my usual rest requirement. No, the dark circles were not from sleep deprivation, but from too much dairy and sugar, consumed in orgy quantities.

One self-observation followed another, such as my tendency to trip on craggy sidewalks and bump toes and knees on objects that are normally harmless. I would forget what I had walked to the other side of a room to retrieve. It was easy to observe similar stress reactions that hundreds of New Yorkers were experiencing. TV coverage was impacting viewers around the country—around the world. Life would never be the same.

Even without the stress of 9/11, the revved momentum that I always felt when maneuvering on the sidewalks of New York continued to pull me into its own kind of unconsciousness. More than once, caught up in the motion and intensity of the crowds, I tumbled to the sidewalk, totally unaware of where I had been placing my feet.

One very cold, wintry day, I walked in such a state to my bank, along an uneven stretch of sidewalk on Thirteenth and Fifth. My boot caught on a piece of packing tape that was splayed on a chunk of sidewalk that had slithered over onto its neighboring piece, the way the tectonic plates move along the San Andreas Fault in California.

I tripped and fell flat on my face, belly and knees, into total darkness. A shaft of light reached me as I gained enough composure to pull back the black wool hat that had fallen over my face. A very round, ruddy face appeared, in its mouth a fat cigar. I heard the exclamation, "Hey, Lady! You okay?"

The man behind the face helped me to my feet and held my arm tightly until I steadied myself. I had flown right into the center of picketing union workers who marched with their placards on behalf of the elevator maintenance rebellion. They warmed themselves, ceremoniously, standing over a contained fire in a city trash barrel just off the curb.

While they all turned their attention my way, one of them dashed into the nearby parking garage office and wheeled out a greasy old desk chair. He shoved it right under me, insisting that I not move until I was sure that nothing was broken.

Having already created a pedestrian-stopping spectacle, I sized up the situation and decided to follow his orders and take inventory. All seemed in place and intact, except for two rapidly swelling goose eggs, one on each knee. After a few moments, I asked the men how their cause was fairing.

"Veh-ree well, tanks." was their proud reply.

Then, slowly, I lifted myself from the chair-on-wheels. I thanked them for their concern and continued, gingerly, on my way.

It came to me that after hearing a daily update from Ground Zero and its resulting aftermath, a major part of *me* had "left the building." A dastardly anti-America campaign had invaded our country. I was not so much feeling fearful, but rather that all of this was bigger than me. I was operating in a way that seemed as though I had relinquished a portion of my own personal, spiritual space to the effects of a force that I know is *not* greater than my connection to a Higher

Power. I truly believe that there is no energy, no one and no thing that is greater.

Distracted by the horror, my spirit continued to vacate my physical premises. I was not fully in my body. Feeling caught in the undertow of mass overwhelm, I let the outer world override my better choices for my sense of wellbeing. Inevitably, I was the one to awaken with those dark circles and dull headaches the morning after unconscious eating. I would have to contend with hobbling about after a spill.

In spite of the wear and tear of living in New York City, I still support the suggestion that everyone should live one year in that city. I once heard the actress Lauren Bacall say, "You can't take the subway in Manhattan every day, and not learn that no one owes you anything!" New York City is where you most certainly learn to take care of yourself.

The city commands a very particular focus that is necessary for survival. It pushes you into your place in line behind those who are speaking one of more than one hundred and forty dialects and languages. The city teaches you humility when you walk the sidewalks alongside hundreds who barely fit there beside you. You stand in line behind millions who seek the same quality of life and success, holding on tightly to their dreams. And most of them are in a tremendous hurry to make it all happen.

Stories of unbridled and overnight successes become mythical fables that are retold in neighborhood pubs throughout the burroughs. Some attain the success—or some version of their dream—with or without happiness and fulfillment. Many return home to simpler and quieter lives. Some remain with the desperate hope of a Las Vegas or Atlantic City gambler; certain that the next performance, manuscript, design, product or "pitch" will procure the big win.

In New York, I had written and sold my second book. I had traveled conveniently from New York to more unimaginable places than from any other place I had ever lived. I had become more street-smart and savvy through more varied experiences than my native California had ever provided. I had grown from challenged perceptions and acceptance of diverse customs, life-styles and manners far different from mine. But now I felt weary and worn.

John Hughes, my coordinator in Australia, who lived between "OZ" and the UK, was very concerned and caring about me, the toll that the city and 9/11 had taken on me. He phoned me from Australia as soon as he could get a working and available phone line. He listened with compassion to the telling of my experience. Then he kindly offered me his home in London in which to regroup before a commitment the following March. Serendipitously, it was a speaking engagement on a cruise ship that sailed out of England.

While I considered his gracious offer, numerous other clear and distinct personal "road signs" led me to the realization that it was time for me to leave New York. In less time than I can account for, all that was to be carried forward from my experience there was packed, shipped or stored. I would decide about my life's next destination from London.

On December 10th, United Airlines lifted me out of New York towards Heathrow. I watched the war-torn city below me, recently challenged by yet another airplane crash. It felt like I was being de-velcroed from (the words that came to mind) the morass and the miasma. Later, I looked up both words in the dictionary, and sure enough, they fit quite appropriately. **Morass**: *a frustrating, confusing or unmanageable situation that makes any kind of progress extremely slow.* **Miasma**: *1. A harmful* *or poisonous emanation, especially one caused by burning or decaying organic matter; 2. An unwholesome or menacing atmosphere.*

Feeling a bit as though I was jumping ship while New York City struggled to stay afloat, I allowed myself a closing reflection of the past weeks. The City *had* become frustrating, with phone cables still not operating properly and too many businesses now defunct or operating at reduced speed, even while the city bravely persevered and rebuilt. Many of us small business owners experienced an amplified version of the country's collective gasp, holding our breath since 9/11. We waited and waited for a unified *exhale*.

The miasma of New York had continued to feel intrusive and pervading. The wind had blown the horrible debris towards Brooklyn and away from Manhattan on that dreadful day. One day, the wind shifted and blew in our direction. Herds of us residents who lived or walked south of Fourteenth Street scurried to Rite Aid and Duane Reade Drugs in search of surgical masks. There were none left and clerks promised to reorder. Although the smoky haze was now contained and hovering around the excavation site. I still felt something thick, oppressive and inescapable in the air.

All the while the city was becoming more compassionate and yielding—even the cab drivers.

Everyone had more patience with those who simply needed to talk, myself included. I was finding greater allowance from fellow passengers whenever and to wherever I traveled after 9/11. We now all found ourselves in the same boat—or plane—of delays, long security lines, reschedules and jumpy passengers. On trips out of the city, I was finding that even with new luggage restrictions, others waited more patiently when I hoisted my overloaded carry-on into the overhead bin and scrunched my computer backpack (now combined to include purse contents) at my feet. I felt part of a distinctly kinder brotherhood and sisterhood of humanity.

Shortly before my departure, I made my final farewell walk down to Ground Zero. The surreal specter of the Twin Tower skeleton still reached to the heavens, having delivered its human offering to God. It remained in a smoky mist, backlit by the eerie light from the tireless, ongoing demolition. I felt, even still, an atmosphere of shock and unearthly confusion. I breathed in what continued to feel like the unhealthy air of pulverized debris of glass, aluminum, asbestos, plastic and I-cannot-allow-myself-to-imagine what else. I said my prayers, thanked all the souls who sacrificed their lives for the spiritual awakening of so many and said goodbye.

In the months that followed my departure and my move to London, I became aware that I had left something else behind in New York City, however—something that changed my future in critical and profound ways, forever.

Introduction

"Tell me my future!"

Nothing makes me want to run faster and farther than hearing those four little words. I am not a short-order cook responding to, "Gimme a ham 'n cheese and make it quick!" The term, "fortune telling" conjures up images of gypsies and carnival shysters. This stereotype used to make me hesitant to call myself a psychic or to divulge too much information about my intuitive gifts. In spite of the fact that I spend much of my professional life on the edge of this three-dimensional reality, the emphasis of my work focuses on the here and now. This more "grounded" style has helped to dispel some pretty goofy assumptions about me and the nature of what I do.

In my childhood, I sensed things that others did not. Many children lose their intuitive abilities when parents chastise them or dismiss multi-sensory gifts. Fortunately, my own gifts remained intact. This was probably due to the unconditional love and ongoing spiritual support that I received from my mother.

At four years old, I shared a precognitive sensing with her. I told her that when she went to heaven, we would "write letters." After her passing at fifty-one, we communicated on a regular basis through thoughts and dreams.

Years later, when my own daughter was four years old, she told me about a conversation that she had with my mother, the grand-mother whom she had never met in the physical realm. While my daughter played in her closet, my mother told Adrianne the details of a private joke, known only to Mother and me.

My mother often had precognitive dreams. My father told entertaining stories involving psychic occurrences with his mother and grandmother. No one in the family had judgments about psychics or paranormal phenomena. We simply had no reference to that sort of sensing. It all floated around in a sort of *Twilight Zone.*

A psychologist once hypothesized that I am able to merge with another's consciousness because I was born a twin. Maybe she figured that I practiced getting into my twin brother's head when we were hanging out in the womb. While that explanation may have satisfied her, I know better. There is more involved than prenatal interaction with my "womb-mate."

Like many highly intuitive people, I have always been atten-tive to minute details in my physical world. I can still envision the cracks on the walkway outside the back door of my childhood home where I used to roller-skate. It drives me crazy when I sleep beneath a ceiling finished with sprayed dry wall. I cannot escape seeing things in all the bumps and crevices. The bedroom ceiling in my first marriage was crowded with the images of a deer head, an old woman, her cat and an aardvark. They shared the ceiling space with the silhouette of "DJ, Dishonest John," the puppet character from *Beany and Cecil*, which was my favorite TV show in the 1940s.

As I got older, I did not realize that I was unintentionally merging with the consciousness of others. In doing so, I was also taking on their emotions. If I stepped onto a bus with a sense of optimism, I might exit feeling quite depressed. While sitting on the bus, absentmindedly looking around at the other passengers, I might "see" that one woman was going through a divorce. Another was beyond frustration with her teenage son. The man across the aisle had just lost his job. Little wonder that I would step off the bus feeling disheartened and discouraged, thinking, "What's the use?"

Later on, I learned to meditate through the Transcendental Meditation movement in the early seventies. I was invited into the advanced course with the condition that I promise not to use my psychic gifts. They explained their need for a policy that filters out "New Age" influences that are considered "fringy" or (in my own estimation) downright silly. I agreed with their philosophy, but had to decline their invitation. I could not separate myself from my gifts.

During that time I also joined a metaphysical class and read a lot of inspiring books. I learned to fine-tune my abilities and access them on demand. Equally important, I learned to turn them off. It was mandatory for me to avoid picking up information on people every minute. Once I was able to control the way

I received intuited information, my focus shifted to developing clearer and more concise methods of interpretation.

I am elated when my apprentice "enlistments" receive unmistakable confirmation that they themselves are receiving highly intuitive information. I help them customize their own "templates" in which to sort out and interpret what that they receive in their own unique style.

When apprentices express their delight with direct "hits," I respond, "Indeed! You *are* a powerful receiver. We are *all* meant to be receivers. So, now ... what exactly, are you going to *do* with the information?"

I coach apprentices in interpreting and decoding images and symbols. The client needs to hear a variety of interpretations, demonstrating that there is no one absolute translation of non-linear information. I believe that psychics do a great disservice when they give the impression that it is within their all-knowing power to interpret information with unquestionable certainty.

It is far more empowering for the client to receive a variety of interpretations, for two reasons: 1) There is an entrainment effect that actually pulls clients into the frequency of perceiving non-linearly. Witnessing the behind-the-scenes interpretation of information furthers their own multi-sensory development; 2) Clients are less likely to obsess about the information given in a consultation—particularly involving the future—when they are shown several possible meanings. This allows them to experience for themselves the marvelous way in which the Universe communicates directly through images and symbols, sometimes only to make sense over the passage of time.

There must be an emphasis on interpreting intuited information in ways that expand, enlighten and empower clients. It is crucial that the client be left at a higher level of understanding. Information must be presented in a way that prompts life-enhancing, life-expanding insights—relevant to life in the present, rather than serving as entertainment that diverts clients from their personal challenges.

The ego-self occasionally tempts my apprentices to become a roadside attraction and to show off their gifts. "Ego-fluffing" is a certain way to delay their journey, particularly as an intuitive. I remind them that it is becoming less remarkable these days to be a multi-sensory receiver. These gifts are intrinsic to the species that we are *all* destined to become.

It is crucial to trust a new way of interacting with your outer world. It involves a more intricate way of interpreting a higher, two-way communication with the Universe. To this end, people are beginning to wake up to their own multi-sensory, intuitive gifts. I am deeply dedicated to supporting a greater trust of these gifts in others.

My work as a clairvoyant, time-traveling, intuitive spiritual counselor takes me many places that exist beyond time and death, as well as to interesting physical destinations. Amidst all the craziness going on in our world, I continue to view an abundance of wonderful, positive future moments. Positive "sneak previews" appear to those who are becoming conscious and decisive in their spiritual awakening.

The future moments that I see in consultations have revealed more than one client meeting a healthy partner, holding a rewarding job and resolving unfinished business with honesty and greater integrity. I have seen parents in the future where they are raising "remembering" children in safe and happy homes. These children are reincarnating souls who inevitably recognize people and objects that surrounded them from a previous life space.

During consultations with their future family members and friends, moments of recognition are previewed and projected from these souls *before* their births. You may have experienced one of these souls, embodied as a little niece or nephew who has looked up at you and exclaimed, "Once you were *my* baby!"

These children hit the ground running, arriving as extremely intuitive telepathic visionaries. They sometimes seem wiser for their years than their parents. They are driven by tremendous sense of purpose: to further their soul's expansion, to assist in the healing and spiritual awakening of others, and to participate in a unifying global vision. Their commitment is one that will promote respect for the diversity of cultures, religions and beliefs. They will implement these ideals through the use of their own extraordinary gifts.

I also find myself applauding the many clients who are making more conscious choices in the day-to-day moments of their personal *and* professional lives. They are making intentional choices towards greater growth and understanding in relationships. More deliberate choices are steering them away from addictions. Awakening is moving them through old patterns into more freedom in the present. They are creating new and brighter futures.

I witness incredible soul expansion in clients, sometimes prompted by seemingly insurmountable, life-shifting challenges. This is coming about through the observation and processing of personal issues, often triggered by the turmoil and angst in their outer world. I see many awakened individuals in joyful future moments that represent the outer reflection of this personal inner work.

I have to mention my amazement at how quickly folks are awakening and becoming multi-dimensional. So very many are learning to decipher ongoing guidance from the Universe. They value daily two-way communication with the Source and non-physical dimensions.

I have observed a positive influence that helps others learn to comprehend this kind of communication. It results from audiences watching people like myself interpret for loved ones on the Other Side. John Edward, a medium who hosted the TV program "Crossing Over," is a good example. Clients tell me that we share a similar style of interpretation. I feel that consistently viewing this type of intuitive reception and interpretation entrains individuals into a frequency of transmitting and receiving effectively in their own right.

People are starting to get it. Rather than seeking the kind of evidence that the rational mind craves, they sense the way that we interpret subtle images and symbols. This is a dramatic shift from the more concrete, mental ways of perceiving. As a result, they are leaving behind old, traditional, counter productive demands for quantifiable physical evidence of the existence of life after death, telepathy and our ability to perceive beyond time.

People are moving out of their heads and into their hearts. This is truly exciting for me to witness. I am fully prepared to assist in ushering forth a whole new wave of highly intuitive individuals who will reach far beyond my own capabilities.

Glossary

Here is a description of my own personal terminology, which I use for interpreting information that I retrieve clairvoyantly. It will serve as a sort of glossary to clarify references that I make throughout this book.

A "**bleedthrough**" occurs when specific traits, talents, characteristics or unfinished business from past lives seep into the client's present "life space." It is often experienced as a fleeting memory or flashback. It reminds me of the effect achieved when I work with images on the computer in Photoshop. I can select the option "bring back to front." In a similar way, an aspect of a past life space seems to come forward into the client's present life space. For example, I might see evidence of primitive Native American aspects in a client that are bleeding through into the present space. The client is likely to become more attentive to nature and feel greater awe for its miracles. Or, for the first time in his life, he might decide to plant a garden and then discovers that he has a green thumb. Or, the client might be on the verge of regaining a renewed and deep respect for The Great Spirit.

"**Checking in with headquarters**" is my personal expression for meditating.

"**Life spaces**" is my particular reference to what others refer to as "past lives." Beyond the illusion of time, we co-exist in other life spaces. From the limited view of the third-dimensional, linear world, one lifetime *seems* to occur before another. In actuality, the soul embodies an awareness that transcends "before" and "after." However, for the sake of clarity, I will refer to life spaces in a sequential manner.

A "**no-time zone**" is where I spend much of my professional life. It is the state of retrieving information that exists beyond the illusion of linearly perceived time. Projections from souls who are preparing for "re-entry," and those who project from the "Other Side" are not limited by linear time constraints. These souls exist in a "no-time zone" as well.

"The Other Side" is a popular term I am forever reiterating that it is *not* a place, but rather a state of continuing consciousness through which non-physical souls project images from the non-physical dimension.

"Over-soul over-ride" is my reference to a specific type of occurrence. When we experience a higher aspect of our consciousness communicating through ourselves, its message tends to override the personality self. This can happen consciously, when words of extreme clarity or profundity flow right through us. When it happens to me, I want to say, "Somebody write that down!" Other times, there might be little or no conscious awareness of this streaming communication. For example, Maryann is a client who offered me her house in Connecticut at the beginning of a U.S. tour, at a time when I needed to relocate from London back to the States. At the onset of that trip, I had the intention to resettle back in the U.S., but had not yet determined where. Maryann swears that she does not remember saying to me, "Please, come do my consultation at my house. See if you might eventually be living there." That is precisely where I moved at the end of that tour, following my two years in London.

"Past-life overlays" is the way I describe scenes from another life space. They coalesce with something going on in the client's present. It is as if a previous event, personality characteristic, talent or unresolved challenge floats in over the client's present life space. It appears to me as a sort of double exposure.

A **"Reading in the Round"** is a group of ten who assemble, usually in a hotel or private home. This is a more intimate setting than the spot "tuning-in" that I accomplish in large audiences. In the RIR, I work with individuals by helping them process issues as they naturally arise in the session. As I go around the circle, I describe scenes as they appear in my no-time zone. Utilizing this information, I re-position the participant in the past. Then, I re-frame his/her life in the present. Finally, I "pull a thread" to the future. From there, I look around and relay the probable future outcomes facilitated by these shifts. The RIR is a fun experience, often deepened by supportive messages from departed loved ones.

"Re-entry" is my term for reincarnation, the rebirth of a soul into another physical body. Souls projecting from the non-physical dimension often indicate that they will be returning as a "remembering" soul. They often send "sneak previews"—scenes that represent future glimpses of specific future moments that are certain to occur after their birth. These are moments of rec-ognition of certain objects or memories carried from another life space. When I relay this information to expectant parents, they validate that those moments have indeed occurred. Most often, this phenomenon occurs within two months to five years of age of the reincarnated soul.

I have a program in which I work with **apprentices** around the world, helping them become more effective receivers of highly intuitive information. We work together over the phone and in "Intensives" conducted at my home. Clients are invited into the program when they have the desire and focused inten-tion to "enlist," and I feel that my coaching will help them expand and refine their intuitive abilities.

I want to mention a few words about terminology, since the words that I choose will have certain meaning to the reader. This is particularly true when they relate to important, personal beliefs.

I am respectful of the fact that my clients—and my readers—hold many differing religious and spiritual beliefs. Individuals refer to a Supreme Being in a variety of ways.

For example, I find that my religious Jewish clients refer to the concept of a Supreme Being as "Hashem" (meaning, "the name"). This is done so as not to diminish the greatness that it represents by even uttering the name of "G-d." My Native American clients call God "The Breathmaker," while Muslims praise "Allah." Some feel that referring to "God" connotes religious dogma. I tend to use "The Source" and "God" interchangeably.

I cordially invite you into my world with the hope that you might see your life from a whole new perspective. Your world—and your future—will never look the same again. Stepping into my shoes will help you trust your own emerging intuitive gifts.

ONE

The Fantasy of the Future

> "You can see only as far as your headlights, but you can make the whole trip that way."

> —E.L. Doctorow

Future Dreams

It is not unusual to envision a future in which you are playing the perfect part in a script that is written and directed by yourself. A cast of characters adores you and reflects back your most prized attributes. A perfect partner might reside there. Your children have matured and are finding their way. And some form of a metaphorical ship sails in, bearing abundance, creative inspiration, spiritual enlightenment and unlimited fulfillment. No matter what is occurring in the present, no matter what has challenged you in the past, that future remains an idyllic constant that will compensate or reward you for all that has come before.

An unexpected event can change your world. It can fortify the illusion of your future as a "fantasy island" to where you escape when unfathomable events or extraordinary disappointments make present reality intolerable.

Advertisers and scriptwriters promote a lifestyle that extols conspicuous consumption, feeding an insatiable standard. Our fantasies are often fueled by these images, which we carry around in our cache of thoughts. The message we learn is that you will never have all that you need. Everything is always out of reach.

Over time, a society so influenced by beliefs in limitation and lack will perpetuate a sort of group mind. This "consensus reality" has the effect of disconnecting you from present and vital truths that bear marvelous gifts.

Consensus reality positions you to romp in this playground of illusion until life jars you awake by loss, tragedy or misfortune. Then you start to ask important questions, sometimes from a sense of deep despair or disillusionment. This is a good thing. It indicates a disengagement from the illusion. It represents a break from playing at life in a sandbox of duality: good guys/bad guys, he said/she said, judging events and people in terms of black and white absolutes.

When you are always looking to the future, you have your back to the door through which serendipitous cues and subtle messages flow. You miss this Divine communication that is intended to lead you toward a happier, more fulfilling life.

The more you become aware of this influence, the more you will be able to integrate your life's desires into a healthier, attainable reality. The effect is extremely empowering. Through the years I have consistently counseled clients to release their expectations regarding future partners. For example, I caution the client who laments that past lovers never sent roses. Her expectations of a rose-bearing partner in the future might cause her to dismiss the divinely designated one: the one due to arrive with a bouquet of daisies.

A perfect "ten" in another client's dreams might appear, sporting the perfect body, but with few gifts that will serve either of them well in relationship or soul growth. On the other hand, such a meeting can serve as a valuable awakening to the lack of fulfillment that results when our hearts' desires are determined by the ego-self. Such experiences usually provide abundant grist for the soul's mill. There is no judgment as to how long it takes to awaken to soul-evolving insights.

On the other hand, there are those whose paths steer them away from the restricting influence of consensus reality. Approval from others does not rule them and they are propelled by their own passion into unique endeavors and even eccentric lifestyles. These people live with a greater degree of freedom than the rest of us.

Personally, my life was primed to be shaped by consensus reality. I grew up near Pasadena, California, not far from Hollywood and a short distance from Disneyland. I loved the special dates when boyfriends were old enough to drive me to Grauman's Chinese Theater in Hollywood. We would drive alongside the "fast" crowd on Sunset Boulevard, watching the parade of customized hotrods.

I read movie magazines, swooned over Troy Donahue and truly believed that the life of Mouseketeer Annette Funicello had to be blessed. My heart fluttered over the twin brothers on the cover of Seventeen Magazine. I ached for a reply to the fan letter I sent them. Having a twin brother of my own, I was convinced that our mutual state of "twindom" would join us in a fabulous future. I addressed my letter to the collective twins. I would have taken either one.

That experience symbolized the embracing of a false belief: Whatever I truly desire in life will never be mine. I never realized that what appears to be out of reach is rarely good for me. It is just so much illusion, and illusion masks all that is for my highest good. That which is destined to serve me well is often right under my nose. That which the Universe dispatches to my doorstep will *always* look different from my expectations.

For many years I traveled my path, distracted and alienated by so many of my own illusions. For example, after my divorce I fantasized that I would achieve true happiness in life if only I could take a cruise around the world. Subsequently, over the years I have been invited to speak on several cruise ships. While I appreciate the opportunity to travel to interesting places, enjoy a delightful change of scenery, make presentations to new audiences and meet new clients, I personally would not choose a cruise for my own leisure adventure. I find that cruise ships comprise big floating hotels with too much food. My dream dissolved when it became reality. The result was less frustration about all that my life did not contain and a reprioritizing of future desires.

An earth-shaking, life-changing realization came to me in the middle of the night, two days before the earth did actually tremble on September 11th, 2001. The wake-up call was presumably staged to jar me from one of my greatest illusions. In retrospect, I see that the message was delivered in a way that would give me an unmistakable assurance that some personal choices to be made after 9/11 had not been influenced by fear. Fear-based decisions are usually the really dumb ones that take us nowhere, and can even result in devastating outcomes. They are derived neither from clear thinking nor divinely inspired guidance.

As clearly as I might have heard someone speaking next to me on my bed, I was awakened that night by *"The Voice"* announcing, *"It's JOHN!"* Never having doubted my two-way communication with the Source, I sat up in bed, thinking through my revolving prayer list. Surely this was not, at long last, the reply to my ongoing bedtime prayer, "Who is my future partner?" Reflexively, I thought to myself, "Maybe if I just go back to sleep, my future partner won't be John." In the four years that I had known John, visions of a Pierce Brosnan-like future partner continued to dissuade me from John's very real and caring overtures. Past illusion programming continued to mislead and frustrate me.

My own life was changed forever two days later when I witnessed the September 11th disaster from my rooftop. As the Towers came down, so did many of my personal illusions. Watching the surreal spectacle shattered my fantasies and plunged me into stark reality. My past presented itself for revision; the present revealed amazing insights and a new future began to unfold within a day of the horrific experience.

On September 12th John called from Australia to express his love and concern for me. He was worried about my continuing to live in New York and invited me to "regroup" at his birthplace in London. John's mother had recently passed away, leaving him the house. All this occurred shortly after the death of John's wife.

Considering the ongoing emphasis with which I caution clients about obsessive soul mate hunts, I shudder to think of them knowing the extent of my own misguided illusions regarding my own future partner. Then again, it is well accepted among students of metaphysics that we do, indeed, "teach what we ourselves need to learn." It took a monumental catastrophe to awaken me from these fantasies.

I had received my very distinct and direct message from the cosmos. Its implication, however, felt far from heavenly. I tried to open up to the love that John was extending, but being on the receiving end felt quite unfamiliar and extremely uncomfortable. I nearly backed out of his kind invitation in more than one fearful moment, confused and overcome with self-doubt. Still, I surrendered to the Source, calling out, "Show me what I need to know about this, *gently* this time!" Every time I did, one more door would open and further reveal the path that led to my marriage to John.

To surrender to John's love was to take me out of a very safe zone. No longer could I could control a future, illusionary partner, one that I could draw any way that tickled my fancy: handsome, clever, mind-reading, humorous, wealthy, charismatic, brilliant and wise. I liked to imagine a relationship with plenty of time for wonderfully stimulating conversations—all of which of course would confirm my own particular point of view on any topic.

But, I had also asked for a partner who would love to cook and to nurture me, leaving me inspired and free to write profundities. I asked for a man who would be supportive of my work, yet not be New-Age goofy. John presented those last two qualifications, most definitely. Other qualities continue to emerge over time, in their own unique, and sometimes challenging, variations.

When lingering illusions cloud the present, I repeat my request: that I be shown what is real and true. Invariably, I then see John or an annoying situation through a new lens.

Sometimes John himself surprises me with a loving gesture that demonstrates a great teaching to me.

Our relationship is a work in progress. Cultural and background differences pose a constant challenge and require a patient and accepting attitude. Regardless of where this path leads us, I am committed to a future that I cannot control. My future certainly "ain't what it used to be!" It has become far greater and more imaginative than I could ever have designed. I married and lived in London. Who knew?

Currently, John and I are separated by "the big pond." It became necessary for me to return to the U.S. to be more active in my work. I will forever be grateful for the loving oasis that John created for me in his unique and caring way. As we both continue to surrender to a bigger plan, I am mindful of one of my own favorite sayings, "You never know what's for what!"

Surrender to the unknowable. Resist the temptation to control the future. When you receive "sneak previews" from intuitives in consultations or from your own "hits," avoid imposing your own egocentric interpretations.

A very different and limitless future awaits you, once you drop the expectations and illusions that trot alongside you from the past, influenced by consensus reality. A divinely customized future will be yours—one that will truly be for your highest good.

Dancing with the Illusionary Self

I observe a predictable progression of insights that come to those who awaken to their true spiritual nature. Lives shift and change with an increased ability to witness life from the perspective of the soul in a non-judgmental way. I laughed when a very multi-dimensional, talented apprentice told me that she often awakens, wondering, "Am *me* today or am I just watching?"

To be "multi-dimensional" is to perceive symbols and images beyond our three-dimensional experience. This includes an ability to see our lives in the context of a much larger plan as it unfolds.

Through conscious observation of self, we become *self*-aware and better able to objectively observe what the ego projects. That is, we become able to watch the role that our personality-self plays in life. As the observer, we become aware of unconscious patterns that influence most of our choices. We begin to notice the triggers that dictate our habitual responses. We experience a dramatic shift from thinking, "*He's* the problem," to "Golly, I had no idea that *this* guy reminds me of my abusive *stepfather!*"

Integrating such observations, the personality-self dominates less and yields to "over-soul over-ride." We find just the right words to express ourselves in the most authentic way. A marvelous flow of events is allowed to unfold. Glimpses of a master plan are revealed through synchronistic events, those that harmonize with the Source and support a timeless design. On that level of perception, we discover our true identities.

Seeing and experiencing life in this way allows the darkness to become useful and constructive when it provides a contrasting backdrop that makes the Light distinct. This is how we discover "that which I am (in Light), by that which I am not (in darkness)." We gain this clarity by reflecting upon some of the really silly—sometimes, ghastly—choices that we made along the way. So often, in challenging moments, I have said, "I can't *wait* for retrospect!" In this more conscious, observer mode, we learn from our mistakes. This is how we become wiser beings.

Challenges bear wise teachings and incredible gifts, as we evolve through them and grow. Rather than having to learn from repetition, we learn from illuminating insights. Old themes stop repeating in our lives.

This is a common scenario: A woman attracts an emotionally unavailable man. In the end, the relationship falters and they break up. Then, she starts dating another emotionally unavailable man. Finally, she observes how she has been attracting men who act like her father. The theme stops repeating.

If the woman takes a breather after the first break-up and resists the urge to jump into the next relationship, she might do some important soul-searching. She will come to important realizations sooner, without having to go through boyfriend number two, three and four.

Those who challenge us the most become our greatest teachers. However, as we begin to learn our lessons sooner through the observer self, we begin to attract fewer perpetrators that tempt us to play the victim. They are no longer necessary.

New and enlightening perspectives replace the ego-self's need to be right. For example, I have observed how the polarizing effect of politics can cause people to hold tight to a particular opinion. I am prey to this tendency, myself. I will cut myself off from new information that might threaten my particular position on an issue and dare to make me wrong. By resisting this tendency, I am free to consider other perspectives and relate better to others with differing beliefs. I prefer to have my position challenged and to be well-informed, rather than having to be *right*.

Consensus reality affects you less as your personal truths become clearer to you. It also becomes easier to speak and live those truths. Your spirit simply will not flow where truth and integrity do not reside. Old friends who continue to base their lives on consensus reality no longer fit into your life. It becomes too difficult to find common ground on which to interact with them. As they begin to fade away, more space opens up for friends who resonate at this new frequency.

Wiser choices become easier to make as we define ourselves less by our external reality. We move away from our need for outer confirmation and gravitate toward a deeper level of self-trust. At that level there is less noise and distraction from external sources.

Internal wisdom becomes more valued than external power. The singular, driven pursuit of material wealth becomes a distraction. Television shows such as *The Apprentice* fuel the motivation for these kinds of pursuits. While the adventures may be fun to watch, would you actually choose to emulate this approach in real life?

A conscious observer mode alleviates the frenetic need to acquire possessions and points us toward greater serenity. Increased serenity heals addictive consumption. We stop buying impulsively when there are fewer emotional voids to fill.

Awakened souls accept the beauty and aesthetics in their outer lives as the natural reflection of the wholeness, clarity and love within. Possessions cease to represent personal worth. Elegant simplicity replaces clutter and creates space for much more that is meaningful and vibrant.

The observer self makes us aware of situations when our personal choices are overly influenced by the expectations of others. Living for others' approval can become an unbearable weight. The ability to observe oneself unveils personal issues. This alerts us as to what is ours—and *not* ours—to fix. Subsequently, this frees us to make choices from a deeper sense of our own truth.

Embracing our pain—and growing from it—clarifies our own personal boundaries. Then we are able to empower others with our faith in *their* ability to heal *themselves*. No longer do we rush to rescue them from their pain. Doing so is often an attempt to end our own discomfort and fear of feeling something similar. A strategic pause allows Divine energy to stream through and show the most inspired way to proceed.

To view my clients' lives from a broader perspective is to help them make sense of the seemingly senseless. Receiving confirmation that a bigger picture is unfolding might not ease the pain of a present crisis. However, the ongoing awareness of it will eventually give meaning to the bizarre twists and turns of the journey.

At first glance, so many of my clients' lives could easily be dismissed as crazy and chaotic—meaningless—with too many mean and painful things happening all too often. In our sessions, we find hidden value and a clear purpose in their lives that lift them out of disappointment and a sense of betrayal.

We also take note of the influences of consensus reality. We identify the influences that cause them to respond reflexively to shallow trends in their lives. We differentiate between what is significant and what is inconsequential. After that, the client begins to move on from "dancing with the illusionary self."

Over the years, a few clients and friends have shared some of their own past illusions with me. Looking back, they see the influence of consensus reality:

Diane is a friend who related her version of having lived most of her married life with certain expectations. She was continually unhappy because of all that she believed herself to be missing. So much seemed out of reach in her marriage and personal life. After her divorce she took the time to explore personal issues and allowed herself some time alone. Eventually she started to draw life-enhancing events and opportunities into her life.

She laughed at how her fantasies had changed since that time. She was amazed at the insights she gained as she reflected on that period of her life. One realization was that she had always believed that she needed a formal dinner setting for twelve for those large, elegant dinner parties. Life was now emphasizing a need to lighten her load. It was an extremely freeing and enlightening exercise. The circumstances surrounding an unsatisfactory financial divorce settlement forced a shift in her priorities. At times, this proved to be a very uncomfortable awakening, but one that caused her to take note. She realized that she rarely had more than two or three friends to dinner.

Emily is a friend who grew up in the South. She confided her favorite fantasy to me. She would imagine that she was attending an elegant ball, one that is right out of the movie *Gone With the Wind*. She envisioned herself dressed in an exquisite ball gown, being waltzed around the dance floor in the arms of a handsome man. In her fantasy, she would stop, suddenly, to look at the face of the mystery man. Was it Clark Gable? Gregory Peck? Or maybe more recently, Richard Gere . . . or Brad Pitt? (She must have known that Pierce Brosnan was *mine!*)

One day she said, "I was recently shocked to be playing my fantasy, only to discover myself dancing in the arms of my own husband!" I commented that I thought that she was evolving beyond her illusionary self, no longer to dance with the fantasies that shaped so many of her dreams.

At the time, I was living in Colorado. I discovered that my own illusions covered such minutia as thinking that I always needed a halter jumpsuit for those summer barbecues. Taking a closer look, I realized that I had been to only one barbecue in twenty years and it took place in the mountains, in the winter. Little wonder that reality had to nearly hit me with tons of concrete to awaken me to greater realizations and move me beyond old fantasies. I left very different expectations of my future behind when I left New York City.

The Impermanence of All Things

It is particularly enlightening to confront the impermanence of all things. We tend to feel a false sense of safety when life stays the same for any period of time. We delude ourselves by thinking that we can keep change at bay and avoid its disruptions if we simply focus on securing everything in its place and diminishing our imperfections. We seem to believe that by making things more perfect in the present, we will safeguard certainties, decrease uncertainties and secure for ourselves a personally endorsed future.

When I observe how frantically we do this at times, I am reminded of an account I once read from a young man who emerged, remarkably, from autism. He had the ability and clarity to reflect on how it felt to have experienced life as an autistic child. He described a memory of lying on the floor, feeling obsessively driven to count each strand of shag carpet, fearful that if he stopped for one moment, his whole world would collapse. In a similar but less extreme way, we expend tremendous energy bracing ourselves against change. We busy ourselves with minutia in order to avoid the unexpected. This prohibits our release into the fullness and flow of life.

When we access a quieter place in ourselves, we are less dependent on sameness in our outer world. We are less desperate for that illusionary sense of safety. When we resolve that nothing stays the same and that we are ultimately powerless to control our lives or the people around us, we are free to flow with unexpected and welcome new adventures.

For example, I have found that my own practice of "checking in with headquarters" (meditating) and yielding to guidance from the Source (dropping my own agenda) allow me to be receptive to the directives that I receive periodically, which guide me to each new living destination. Up until my nearly eight years in New York City, these moves tended to occur about every three years.

When I am given notice of imminent relocation, it usually happens with little warning. I receive a clear vision, knowing or sudden shift in perception that instantaneously shifts my reality altogether. Then unmistakable road signs appear. The move always unfolds gracefully and flowingly. This is how I can be certain that I am following guidance and making the right move.

Moving to new locations instills the truth about the impermanence of all things. Nothing stays the same and life is ever changing. Change brings new insights about myself. Sometimes I am forced to access new strengths in myself that I had yet to discover. Change also connects me to new people and places that sometime trigger unfamiliar emotions in me. I am compelled to take a closer look at what I have yet to heal in myself.

Everyone ought to make a move now and then. Moving forces you to lighten your load and pull out of energetic stagnation. It can be the positive side of a job transfer. Unfortunately, children of families who are always on the move, such those in the military, are often left to contend with the psychological impact of lacking roots and a trust in deeper relationships. However, this is referring to an extreme.

Not only is moving is an excellent exercise for realizing the impermanence of all things; it also challenges us to "bloom wherever we are planted," a great spiritual challenge. In times ahead, we will all need to pay attention to personal guidance, which will lead us to optimal locations that are for our highest good.

Our vital lifeline through change is our intimate connection to the Source. Through this ever-changing flow of life, alternative and far more creative routes are revealed. I experienced a shift in my own life years ago, when my attitude changed regarding the impermanence of all things. It came to me through two different, contrasting experiences, twenty years apart.

It was in my early twenties, after the passing of both of my parents. I took a trip to La Cañada, the town where I grew up. I wanted to pay homage to the place where I had spent my first eighteen years. I will never forget my feelings of sadness and frustration when I saw the house that my father had forever been improving.

The house was now painted a dingy brown. The front lawn was unkempt, colored a rusty brown. I looked down into an adjoining area—"the park"—where my brothers and I used to play baseball, kickball and tag. Clinging to inner tubes suspended from an old oak tree, we would shriek with delight and fear when we swung down into it. The area was now subdivided. All the trees were gone. Four houses invaded the property where we had romped and played.

"Can't *anything* stay the same?" I lamented to myself, feeling the tremendous void left from my parents' passing. Suddenly, I missed them terribly.

Later, in my forties, I was living in an old apartment on Lakeshore Avenue in Oakland, California. It was a wonderful, funky old apartment from the 1920s, with high ceilings, vintage glass doorknobs and beautiful hardwood flooring. Large bay windows overlooked Lake Merritt.

One weekend, a movie crew was filming *Made in America*, staring Ted Danson and Whoopie Goldberg. Throughout those couple of days, I walked around the lake to watch the production.

Behind the lake, the vacant space across from the public library had been transformed into a used car lot. A tall wooden cutout of a cowboy salesman waved in prospective customers. One end of the lake had been dredged to create the illusion of a beach. Before my eyes, I saw the movie people create a whole different reality.

I watched Ted Danson fall off a runaway elephant into the lake. I saw the camera crew carefully choreograph Whoopie's double as she rode recklessly through a congested intersection on a bicycle. I felt sympathy for the forty extras that were directed to run after her, shaking their fists furiously in the air. They had to repeat the scene at least as many times as they numbered.

On Monday, I took a lunch break and walked back to that end of the lake. There was no trace of the world I had seen created before my eyes. The illusion was gone. With surprise, I took note of my feeling of tremendous relief as I allowed myself to experience my world as ever changing.

Over the years, something had grown in me, something that now anchored me deeper within myself and to the Source. I felt less need to reach to things external, temporary and transient. Granted, a lack of attachment to a movie set can hardly compare to the longing for the place and time of my childhood. But I noticed that the ache for steady, predictable sameness was most definitely a diminishing one.

Years ago, a message came through for one of my earliest classes: *"In these times, that by which you define yourself will be gone, so that you can truly know who you are."*

I observe more and more people who experience greater peace and freedom when they become anchored to life in this deeper, less externalized way. Material possessions and approval from others no longer influence their motivation or choices. Their spiritual guidance systems become finely tuned when their hearts align with the Source. Synchronistic events and serendipitous meetings present unmistakable road signs.

When we become the observers of our lives and live in an awakened state, all that is unnecessary and burdensome starts to fall away. Priorities, needs, preferences and fears will shift and change. So does our relationship to the physical world. Our eternal spiritual self becomes more identifiable, and our life's purpose is revealed. We value the lessons that bring realizations and promote growth. We are able to view the bigger picture by trusting intuitive insights. We operate from love instead of fear. It is well worth the journey.

TWO

The Illusion of Time

"It is only in appearance that time is a river. It is rather a vast landscape and it is the eye of the beholder that moves."

—Thornton Wilder

Time does not truly exist, except in the way that we witness it. Through our perceptions we experience still scenes, which are not moving through time. Rather, it is our consciousness moving through these scenes that creates the perception of motion.

Imagine that you are holding the filmstrip of a movie that you are about to thread through an old-fashioned movie projector. As you hold the filmstrip in both hands, you can see that there is a beginning to it—close to where your right hand is holding it—which represents the past. Directly in front of you appear all the frames of the movie that represent the present. At

53

the end of the strip—in your left hand—appear the frames that show the future.

If one frozen moment in time is observed, there seems to be no action, as if you are viewing one frame of the filmstrip. But when you put a series of consecutive frames together, you can see the frozen moments as if they are animated. Pieced together, the frames create a movie. Einstein referred to this as a time-continuum.

It is as if past-present-future all exist at one time, on that single strip of film. To look at the filmstrip itself, the piece of celluloid is not much to see. Then you feed it through the projector and turn it on. The projector shines a light through each frame of the filmstrip and projects an image onto the screen that you can see, clear and enlarged.

The frames appear on the screen, and what you experience and view is your present life. The before and after portions of the filmstrip still exist, but you are only focused on the frames that are being illuminated. Those few frames constitute the space in which you live out your present-moment life experience. Perceiving and experiencing only that one space does not mean that the other life-spaces do not exist. In fact, if you walk behind the projector you can look at the entire film at once.

When we leave the physical body and go to the Light, we are able to look back and reflect upon our lives from such a perspective. Just as all frames of the movie exist simultaneously, so do all moments in time. This continuum of time is an illusion. Time itself is an illusion.

The soul is a timeless energy that is ignited by the spirit. Sometimes, the words "soul" and "spirit" are used interchangeably. I like to distinguish them in this way: "Soul" is the cumulative repository of experience, wisdom and knowledge acquired throughout its evolution. It is the essence of who you are. "Spirit" is the Divine spark that animates the soul. It is the omnipresent force of God, the power from which the soul draws.

I am able to tap into a level of consciousness that allows me to experience all of time. I interpret images and symbols that communicate the adventures of the soul. From where I view this information, it is as if the past, present and future co-exist in one place. I watch the scenes, moving them forward and backward at will. With focused concentration, I am able to pull up past scenes and future possibilities. It is not that I create them. Rather, my consciousness becomes aware of them from the perspective of the Higher Self.

In consultations, I share insights with clients as I view their lives from this vantage point. This process helps them become aware of old patterns and the emergence of future potentials. Consciousness expands and personal realities shift with these changing perceptions. All beings who advance will come to understand how this is possible, be it from expanding consciousness or greater scientific understanding of the true nature of the universe.

Princeton physicist John Wheeler coined the term "black hole" to refer to collapsing stars that crunch not only matter, but the surrounding space as well. There, time comes to an end. "Time cannot be an ultimate category in the description of nature," he declares. " 'Before' and 'after' don't rule everywhere." Certainly this describes the way all of time appears on my visual "radar screen."

We have an intimate relationship with time. It shifts as we change our perceptions of it. Our pasts are still evolving. Our futures are not set in stone; the way that both exist at this moment is relative to our view of the present and past.

The movie *Frequency* was a fun metaphor for this concept. The main character found that by finding the right frequency on his father's old ham radio, he could speak to his father in the past. Every time the father did something in his time to change what he perceived to be the future, he altered reality in his son's present time. Together, they successfully created a corridor beyond time through which they interacted.

In a sense, this is what I am able to do, to "time travel" from the present to the past and future. It is as if I log onto my inner broadband connection and retrieve information that exists beyond linear observations of time. This access also connects me to a continuum of consciousness that exists beyond the illusion of death.

When working with clients, I create corridors from the future, present, past and other life spaces. I do this for the purpose of facilitating healing and empowerment, and to demonstrate how spiritually awakened individuals can do the same. I enjoy demonstrating this ability to large audiences through a less in-depth version of what I accomplish in private consultations.

Standing before the audience, I tune-in to a random participant. I often intuit a specific, troublesome issue that currently exists for that person. Then I pull a psychic thread from the present to a co-existing moment in his/her childhood. Seeing through the eyes of the person's child-self, I view strategic moments where truths were denied and inhibitions were planted. I focus on validating feelings and impressions that were dismissed.

Often, this process initiates an immediate change. A shift in perception in the past sends a wave of transformation to the present. The person experiences greater self-trust, less ambivalence in making decisions, greater confidence and a deeper connection to personal feelings.

Then I pull another psychic thread to the future, merging with the client's timeless consciousness. I experience a moment in his/her most positive, probable future. It is a moment that will have just been influenced by the shift that we initiated in the past.

Transcending Linear Time

I have described the way in which I "time-travel" through the conduit of timeless consciousness, helping to shift my clients' realities. I consider myself to be responsible and dedicated to developing practical applications that help others open up to their multi-dimensional nature.

It often feels as though I spend a large portion of my life in a no-time zone. Doing so, however, does not make me an expert in understanding the science of time. There are those who are much more savvy and quite erudite in their interpretation regarding the relative and non-linear nature of time and the non-local characteristic of consciousness.

Rupert Sheldrake writes about "morphic resonance," theorizing that there is a collective memory throughout nature that is expressed through "morphic fields." These fields are within and around each organism. They shape and influence systems over time, rather than seeing systems as changeless and fixed.

In his book *The Sense of Being Stared At*, Sheldrake explores telepathy in detail as part of our natural "seventh" sense. He explains, "the sixth sense has already been claimed by biologists working on the electrical and magnetic senses of animals." His concept of a *seventh* sense is derived from the idea that telepathy, premonitions and the sense of being stared at seem to be in a different category.

Another valuable resource in my explorations comes from my friend and colleague Peter Russell, the author of *Waking Up in Time*. In this book he refines his ideas expressed in *A White Hole in Time*.

You might often feel that time is somehow speeding up. How can this be? The most obvious cause would be the fact that we are filling in so many more waking hours with "time-saving" devices such as microwaves, e-mail and cell phones. But Russell thoroughly explores the literal possibility of *running out of time!* He demonstrates how throughout civilization, evolution and innovation have continued to accelerate. Greater advances have been made in shorter spans of time.

Russell believes that this acceleration will continue until it reaches a point of "singularity." When this occurs, the rate of change will accelerate and go off the charts. His calculations point toward a profound shift in reality and of consciousness. He concludes that "within a few generations, perhaps within our own lifetimes" this shift will occur.

Terrance McKenna also explores this phenomenon by charting peaks and troughs of innovation throughout history. The Renaissance would naturally constitute a peak and the Dark Ages, a trough. Each peak arrives sixty-four times faster than the previous occurrence. McKenna's calculations of *time wave zero* sync with Russell's general estimate.

Undoubtedly, through expanding consciousness we will eventually find ourselves detached from our linear perception of time. After all, multi-dimensional sensing carries us far beyond it. But here we may have evidence that we could actually run *out* of time!

Through differing methods of calculation, Russell and McKenna both predict the same general time period when that reality-changing shift could occur. More specifically, McKenna calculates the date to be December of 2012. This is also when the Mayan calendar ends and the Hopi prophecies are predicted.

Russell emphasizes the need to prepare by making a more deliberate attempt to disengage from materiality and become more comfortable with uncertainty. The effects of both would support a greater ability to stay "present." Staying in the present calls for an intentional focus of our attention on all that challenges and engages us right now.

The ego-self is calmed when corralled in the present. Fear is reduced and we are less compelled to obsessively seek assurances about a projected future. We get sidetracked when we allow ourselves to entertain continual regret about the past and worrisome speculation about the future.

Russell also reminds us of the urgent need to do everything that we possibly can to save this planet's resources while there is still time, even while we prime consciousness to transcend it. We have a responsibility to pick up after ourselves during our stay as physical beings on the earth plane.

I personally believe that the shift predicted by Russell and McKenna might represent many of the changes that religions prophesize. Scriptures and ancient legends forecast apocalyptic shifts, a Messianic arrival and cataclysmic earth change. Can man define that which has not yet been part of his experience? Perhaps these references are metaphors for the shift to hyper-consciousness.

I sometimes wonder if we will even carry a memory of this existence. When I experience and retrieve information from a more expanded plane of consciousness, I experience being completely there, as if I had never existed anywhere else. It seems likely that a more permanent multi-dimensional shift might catapult us into another dimension altogether. We would experience an entirely different reality, perceiving it as our total and complete one. We might not remember this current reality, in the same way that most people do not have memories of previous incarnations.

I met Dr. Larry Dossey when he was a fellow speaker on a cruise venue. He is a medical doctor who has done extensive scientific research on the power of prayer to remotely heal patients. I was impressed with his humor, his down-to-earth southern manner and his ability to bridge the scientific world and the metaphysical with very clarifying concepts.

Afterwards, I discovered his book *Recovering the Soul: A Scientific and Spiritual Search*. In his book he details the "nonlocal" nature of the mind, meaning that the mind is not confined to the physical body. In his chapter, "The Reach of the Mind," he writes:

> Time awareness is a movement away from a nonlocal sense of time to a contracted, local awareness... Adherence to locality in time—always looking ahead or behind, never dwelling in the moment—has become a morbid obsession.
>
> It has spawned a variety of physical illnesses that we could collectively call "time sicknesses"—coronary artery disease, hypertension, peptic ulcer disease, irritable bowel syndrome, and the vascular headache syndromes

including migraine, to name only a few. In general, any illnesses in which anxiety and excessive time awareness have been shown to play a role belong in this growing category of human maladies.

Finally, he mentions the testing done at the Biofeedback Department at Dallas Diagnostic Association. There, they treat such "time sickness" maladies through biofeedback training. They ask patients to perform a simple task on their initial visit. Patients are requested to lean back in a comfortable chair, relax, close their eyes and announce when a minute has passed.

Dossey reports that *everyone* underestimates the passage of time. A man with coronary artery disease held the record by estimating that a minute ended in twelve seconds. Apparently, biofeedback training expands and elongates patients' sense of time. By their final visit they regularly overshoot the mark, sometimes allowing up to three minutes to pass before signaling the passage of one.

Dossey concludes that retraining the time sense in biofeedback, meditation or other forms of deep relaxation increases the awareness of non-local happenings in one's life. That is to say, these techniques increase the recognition of dreams, visions and intuition.

Similarly, the more you detach yourself from a linear way of relating to situations and obligations in your life, the less you try to fit events into a sequential framework. Your frame of reference expands. Your journey becomes more creative and inspired. You will have time for new adventurous routes and you will reach your destinations more joyfully. Stress and frustration diminish when you are no longer defining yourself by meeting deadlines and trying to beat the clock.

Experience fully what is directly before you, instead of gauging your experience by what time it is. You will find that the present moment will lead you to the next. Then that moment leads you to the next one in the easiest and most creative way.

Perceiving non-linearly, you will eventually find it possible to reach the end of your day having managed to fit in all your errands. You will be amazed that you actually completed additional tasks that would normally push you to your limit. You will wonder how in the world you were able to accomplish it all. You will have moved through your day effectively and without stress, feeling in sync with the natural flowing rhythm of life.

We often complain that we don't have time. Technological wonders that appear to save us time actually seduce us into using up more of our available schedule. Being more present will give you moment-to-moment clarity as to what is truly important to accomplish. Then you can decide what you can allow to fall away to another time or to disappear from your agenda altogether.

When you awaken in the morning, pay attention to the thoughts that enter your head as you anticipate your day. Observe the tendency to sequentially itemize all that you intend to accomplish. These items become your lists, mandated by your projected perception of time. Your spirit does not truly relate to time, nor does it operate joyfully or willingly within linear boundaries.

Feel the day before you expand. See it unfold with plenty of space. Visualize the extra space in which you will accomplish everything. Most importantly, deliberately switch to a non-linear perception of all that lies ahead. Resist the temptation to yield to scheduling and list-making objectives.

Next, scope out all that you need to do and where you need to go in your day. Just briefly scan, as if putting all the items on a radar screen. *Don't make a list!* To do so is to go linear and

Visualize

thereby configure your to-do items in a sequence. This creates a psychic and unconscious impression that diminishes the magic of going beyond time. Instead, visualize dropping all the items into the center of your awareness, rather than laying them out on a timeline. Then let go of your expectations concerning how you think you should work with time or how you should attempt to fit into it! It is important to release thoughts that rush in to nail everything down in a concrete way.

Come back to the present and breathe into the moment. With the next deep breath, relax into the feeling of everything being accomplished at the end of your day. Be there, sensing it in every way, seeing it, feeling it and absorbing it. Then, become aware of your surroundings in the present moment. Be there fully. That moment will usher you into the next moment. From there you will flow into the next moment, and so on. You *will* accomplish everything!

You cannot imagine how this will happen, nor do you need to figure that out. You will not feel stressed from trying to do everything within your timed plan. Try this every morning. Paste a Post-It to your nightstand lampshade to remind you: *Into the circle!* It gets easier and will eventually become an automatic process.

When you allow yourself to move freely in each day, your life falls into perfect order. Events synchronize and present themselves in the right sequence. If you resolve to surrender to the natural rhythm of your spirit, you will open yourself to miraculous ways that events, and ultimately your life, can unfold.

In a very practical way, I do this whenever I walk by my desk and see it piled high with unfinished business. My inclination is to impose a time constraint on myself. I think that I really ought to drop everything and attend to it, even if it means going against a strong pull to do something else at the time—even if my spirit does not seem to naturally be flowing in that direction.

I glance over the desk, visually put it all on my inner radar screen and take inventory of all that needs to be accomplished. Then I take a deep breath, inhaling all that I need to do, then exhale, releasing it all to my Higher Self. I continue on to where I was headed in the first place. When the right non-linear space pulls me back toward my desk, I find myself in the middle of accomplishing it all, thoroughly engrossed, with no conscious awareness of having decided to be there.

Years ago, I experienced dramatic results using this method, which I call the "fishhook" technique. I was living in Manhattan at the time, having just returned from several weeks on the road. My assistant booked several phone consultations on my first day back. At the end of that same day I was supposed to present to the FIONS group (Friends of the Institute of Noetic Science).

Upon awakening that morning, my first thoughts were, "How am I ever going to get through this day!" I observed the stress I was already creating for myself by starting to itemize the impossible list of commitments that lay ahead. Then I remembered to go non-linear.

I scanned the names of all the clients who would be calling, then tossed my image of the speaking engagement into the mix. I dropped the whole day's agenda onto my visualized radar screen. All these obligations appeared like bright green dots of light, floating around freely on my imaginary display panel. Then I went to the future moment that was to occur at six-thirty that evening.

I saw and felt myself standing behind the lectern, about to begin my presentation. Having already decided what I was going to wear, I felt the silk jacket's sleeves on my arms. I could feel the audience sitting before me, expectant, with eager anticipation. In that future moment, I had arrived, feeling rested, prepared and eager to begin. I had flowed through all of the day's events that came before. *Somehow*, I had accomplished everything effortlessly and effectively. Then I let all those future scenes float away and came back to my present moment, ready to begin my day. I reminded myself to *stay* in the present.

Six-twenty-nine arrived that evening and I found myself standing behind the lectern in the old church where the FIONS group was meeting. At precisely six-thirty, I felt the exact moment that I had experienced that morning. There it was, just as I had envisioned it; the precise future moment that I had accessed—or created—earlier that day. The instant was so unmistakable that I felt compelled to stop my introduction and share the occurrence with the audience.

It was as if the fishhook caught, then reeled me in through my day and to my intended destination. All it took that morning was a focused resolve to go nonlinear and toss out the fishhook beyond time.

It might seem impossible to break from your usual manner of getting through each day. Start by observing your tendency to put items on your to-do list into linear time slots. In the next moment, do a mental or visual scan of all that needs to be done. Then put the items on your mental radar screen, and release them. Come back to the present moment and direct your thoughts to whatever is going on around you.

As you take the first step forward into your day, make the effort to focus on one task at time. It is a gradual process. Eventually it will become easy and automatic. You will definitely be in the flow, with your spirit leading the way.

Playing With the Time Wizard

I have a friend who calls on her "Time Wizard." She is aware of the principle of linear time being an illusion, but has a hard time relating the concept to her time-oriented daily life. So she calls upon the Wizard to sort it out for her, whenever necessary.

She first tried this on a day that she had to drive from her home in Santa Fe, New Mexico to catch a plane at the Albuquerque Airport—forty-five minutes to one hour away. She had only twenty minutes in which to arrive, park her car, check in and get seated on the plane. There was no way that she was going to accomplish this in that short period of time.

She called out, "Okay, Time Wizard! I know that this time thing is supposedly not real, but I haven't figured out how it works. Therefore, I'm counting on you to handle this for me!" Once she turned onto the main highway, she found herself driving directly behind a policeman the entire way.

It was as if she acquired a personal escort to prove that she could not have been driving over the posted speed limit. At least not in a linearly operating reality! Somehow, going beyond her perceptions of time prompted a reality shift. She found herself seated on the airplane with a few moments to spare, even though she was unable to account for driving time to the airport.

When you break away from the limitations of linear time, you will also become more intuitive about your life. There is a natural and intuitive rhythm to your attuned, expansive self. Learn to pay attention to it.

For example, it is quite easy to give yourself the suggestion to wake up at a specific time. Plant the suggestion in your mind the night before and sure enough, you will awaken right on time. A very efficient clock resides within you. My internal clock even factors in the few extra minutes that I require in the morning to get oriented and give thanks for a new day. Your internal clock can even serve you better than your watch.

I experienced several years without having to wear a watch or look at clocks. I found that my need to check the time of day fell away naturally as a part of my multi-sensory expansion. I also began to notice that jewelry on my hands and arms felt like interference with the flow of my energy. I programmed my internal clock to wake me up in the morning and get me to my destinations on time. Eventually, however, I did have to put my watch back on. When my travels became too extensive, intrinsic distractions became too un-centering to assure that I would catch a plane on time. This was especially the case when I traveled through different time zones.

I still prefer to use my internal time device. When I need to know the time, I relax and ask my Higher Self to give it to me. It usually comes in very accurately.

Accessing your inner clock is an excellent multi-sensory exercise for you to practice. You can use the same method to intuit what the scales will read before you weigh yourself in the morning. You can "know" the age or birth month of a person before they offer that information. Or, you can let the amount of your purchases float into your head before the cashier hands you the receipt.

By now, it has become clear to me that when I find this kind of spontaneous, intuitive check-in to be inaccurate, it is an indicator that I am a bit off-center. I might not be fully present, anticipating future moments that have yet to arrive or are momentarily out of focus from the distractions around me. All I have to do in those moments is to remember to breathe, relax and ask. Then I take the first "hit" that floats into my head.

Sometimes the answer comes to me as if someone told me the time or sum. Sometimes I will just know what time it is. Other times, I see numbers that appear like a digital clock. Occasionally, I see the time appearing on a round clock, although I have been known to interpret this from the wrong side. For example, I might see it as twenty minutes after the hour, rather than twenty minutes before.

It takes practice to learn to use your internal clock, but it does work. The more you exercise your intuition as a resource, the easier it becomes to trust and the more often you receive accurate information. In the beginning, however, you might want to set a back-up alarm.

Being Here and There

I used to think that "multi-tasking" was equivalent to creative genius. I marveled at my ability to accomplish several tasks simultaneously. However, I eventually began to experience more moments when my brilliance in this area came into question. Sometimes I could not remember whom I had put on hold on my speakerphone. Other times, retrieving two or three other objects for different purposes, I would forget why I had placed a certain book on my desk.

I often observed a difficulty in redirecting my scattered thoughts back to a singular task in the present. Maintaining a fluidity of thought and awareness of life around me became nearly impossible. I have since concluded that it is more of an accomplishment for me to successfully focus on one task at a time in the present rather than to yield to time-defying, multi-tasking impulses. Our world today is full of distractions that can prevent us from living in the present moment.

Our challenge is to be aware of the distractions when they divert our attention. Once noticed, bring your focus back to the center of your original task, and resist the powerful temptation to lose that focus. Ignore the reflexive urge to pick up your cell phone while you are driving your car. Turn away from your computer when you have the next conversation with a friend. Give that person your undistracted, undivided attention.

Your spirit can travel to several places at once in the same way that your thoughts are able to. Once again, consciousness is non-local, non-physical and unrestricted by linear time.

Example: Fran is a client whose mother recently died in a car crash. I reported that her mother, transmitting from the Other Side, said, "And by the way, sweetheart, I know about the dog!" Fran exclaimed, "But I got the dog *after* Mom died!" This was her mother's way of confirming that she maintains a strong connection to her daughter, that she is just a thought— a heartbeat away.

Just then I heard the dog start to bark from somewhere near my client in her home. I sensed that he was behind her in the same room. I continued, "Now your mom is transmitting the message, 'I'll see what I can do.'" Suddenly, the dog stopped barking.

"Wait a sec!" Fran interrupted. "I thought you said that Mom is communicating with us from the Other Side! Now you're telling me that she's in my kitchen?" In response, I quoted from the movie *The Matrix*. I said, "This is a mental projection of your mother's digital self!" (The character in the movie was explaining the holographic appearance of another character.)

In the way that our thoughts can exist in several places simultaneously, so can souls who have ejected from their physical bodies. It is as if they project holographic thought images from their energetically complete, timeless and intact selves. Thought travel and consciousness projection is unlimited.

The Soul Knows No Chronology

"Time is nature's way of keeping everything from happening all at once." Jeremy Rifkin, author of *Time Wars*, found this quote written on a café wall. Indeed, the way that we perceive time in this dimension as living beings causes us to witness events as happening sequentially. I believe that as we expand beyond limited perceptions and yield to the true flow of the non-linear/non-local spirit, we will experience the truth about our own existence: Not only are we eternal, we are timeless.

This means that we will become less restricted by old ideas involving chronological aging. Such externalized perceptions limit our potential for greater vitality and wonderful adventures in our later years. In trusting a deeper place within ourselves—where the soul recognizes truth—we will have greater immunity to the persuasive influence of consensus reality. No longer will we feel compelled to reach for products that make us appear other than we truly are. Sooner than we can imagine, the physical body will have the ability to keep up with the spirit's timeless progression.

Scientists now tell us that they are astonishingly close to discovering what triggers stem cell regeneration. Their research is taking them beyond age retarding-hormones. They are discussing age *reversal*, and estimate that people who are currently in their fifties will live to be one hundred and twenty or more. They predict that the younger generation will live as many as thirty years longer. Sociologists are already pondering the cultural ramifications of such breakthroughs.

We see more relationships that defy traditional chronological expectations with respect to choosing partners. Men and women are freeing themselves from imposed traditional expectations. I met a woman on the Isle of Wight in England who is currently in her eighties. She lives happily with her soul mate, a man who is forty years younger. She confided to a close friend, "A violin is never too old to play."

A few years ago, I was sitting on a swing on the top of a mountain, overlooking a beautiful panorama of green rolling hills. I thought to myself, "How would I see this through the eyes of a child?" I tried to shift my focus and do so. A few moments later, I heard a rustle in the leaves behind me. I turned around and saw a young woman approaching. I invited her to come join me on the swing.

"It's really weird," she said, as she sat down beside me. "When I first saw you from the back, I didn't know if you were a young girl, or a older woman." I laughed, thinking how her remark confirmed the effect of my intention. By experiencing my surroundings through my timeless consciousness, I shifted my energy field and influenced the way she perceived me on an energetic level.

I vividly remember, as a child, staring so long into a mirror that I no longer recognized the face looking back at me. It was as if my soul was looking out from my body—my physical self—pondering, "So *this* is who I am . . . *this* time . . ."

I personally think that we gawk when we drive by devastating car crashes because our personality-selves cannot comprehend what the Higher Self knows: Death is an illusion. Our essential self is eternal, even though our body dies. The Higher Self is in harmony with this contradiction, but the little self—the self of the rational mind—cannot grasp this paradox.

I cringe whenever I hear some people my age or older say, "Wups, there goes another brain cell," when they are unable to remember something. "Stop that!" I tell them. "The cells are *listening!*" Then I share a report I once heard from a neurologist, who said that it's not that we lose brain cells. It's more that in these days of "information overload" it simply takes a little longer to pull up the right file!

To this end, I have programmed myself to retrieve information that I am unable to consciously remember in a given moment. After trying as hard as I can to remember something with my mind, I then release *all* thoughts concerning what it is that I have forgotten. Then tidbits of information float back into my consciousness—like a boomerang.

I have perfected this ability to retrieve unremembered information to within five minutes. The only problem is that when I apply this technique in a social setting, by the time the information reaches me, the conversation has usually moved on to other topics.

At a New Year's Eve party in London, I was trying to remember the name of the actress Lily Tomlin while the guests were chatting about American comediennes. I thought and thought, then suddenly released my efforts and silently commanded that information to float back to me, ASAP!

"It's Lily Tomlin!" I exclaimed to the group. Unfortunately, it was after my famous five-minute delay. "Oh? Uh ... um ... so ... ?" Their looks conveyed a hint of annoyance for my interrupting the current topic.

My little trick involves more than mind over matter. It is an attitude that I practice. It helps me reject learned perceptions about aging. Your body is extremely responsive to your thoughts, beliefs, and perceptions regarding chronological aging. It will be happy to age you accordingly and mirror your limiting beliefs with diminished vitality and greater forgetfulness.

Emphasize your aging self and your body will most certainly give you cause to yearn for the younger years. The irony is that even during those younger years, you were most likely lamenting emerging wrinkles, excess weight and whatever seemed unattainable. With every encroaching year that you live with an ongoing identification to your physical self, your body will feel older.

It does not have to be this way. You can learn to live in sync with your timeless spirit. You will gain important insights from your observation of old habits and nonproductive patterns. You will learn more about yourself from those who trigger certain emotional responses in you. Transformation of old perceptions will increase your capacity to forgive old grievances. Then you are released.

Profound realizations will lead you to greater self-actualization and self-acceptance. Greater self-acceptance will make you glow. Feeling better about yourself, you will feel less need to judge others. Living in greater harmony with yourself and your world will make you younger, no matter how many years you are wearing.

You will find yourself awake and attentive to gifts and discoveries that arrive in each new present moment. You will feel free to receive the wisdom gained from making more life-enhancing, life-expanding, conscious choices. The Universe will commune with you and present all the more wondrous adventures, as long as you inhabit your physical body. You will never feel alone, for your spirit will serve as a vital conduit of your connection to the Source.

I would never have dreamed that my experience of September 11th would be the catalyst for so much self-discovery, personal growth and unanticipated adventure. It was important for me to stay present, release my fears to the Source, continue to "check in with headquarters," and ask for—then follow—the road signs.

THREE

The Portal of the Present

*"Life can be found only
in the present moment.
The past is gone, the
future is not yet here, and
if we do not go back to
ourselves in the present
moment, we cannot be
in touch with life."*

—Tich Nhat Hanh

You are connected to a great and wise consciousness, your Higher Self. Surrendering to it allows a greater plan to override the ego-self's preferences and fear-based agendas. I refer to this effect as "over-soul override."

Over-soul override is a mechanism that allows the Divine plan to superimpose itself over mundane thoughts and events. When this occurs, synchronized events lead you through alternate and easily identifiable choices that support the greatest good for everyone. However, Divine energy can only reach you in the present.

The present is where you must learn to reside. The present opens the portal to your Higher Self, to the Divine and to life beyond time and death. It is the opening through which your multi-sensory gifts are delivered and multi-dimensional perceptions are understood.

"In the now" is the only time in which you can make choices. The present is the only place where you can live with compassion for others, accept individual differences and arrive at mutually inspired resolutions. Inaccurate assumptions and unsuitable prejudices from the past reveal themselves clearly in the present. There, they fall away with enlightened elegance.

Living fully in the present puts you in a position that allows you to recognize intuitive insights that can heal the past. In the process, you derail reactive projections. Released from a reactive mode, you cease to blame others as the cause of your unhappiness. "He's the problem!" is no longer your battle cry. And no longer do you credit external forces as the primary determinant in achieving self-fulfillment. Timeless insights are delivered in dreams and epiphanies are dispatched from the Divine.

The present is the only place to gain access to creative and intuitive solutions that transcend rudimentary answers. This is where you acquire multi-dimensional wisdom that the rational mind can neither retrieve nor accept. It is the opening through which hints revealing a bigger plan are sent. Clues lead you on a treasure hunt through the unexpected, towards imaginative and unusual adventures. You must, however, accept that life *will* differ from your own expectations.

The unexpected is *not* an indication of life going wrong, no matter how much those events might challenge you. In the context of the bigger picture, events arrive right on schedule, and that larger scheme reveals itself in the present.

The present is a portal through which to access the magic of the Universe. Only in the present can you observe and enjoy the uncanny way that the Universe instructs with metaphors. Only in the present are you engaged by its outrageous and clever humor, woven throughout the magnificent design of life.

Quite often, our unreasonable, unattainable expectations of perfection become obsessive and divert us onto tedious side roads. Being in the beam of Divine energy makes it easy to pause . . . and allow insightful observations to get us back on track.

Living with linear perceptions is like having your back against the very door through which the Universe delivers infinite possibilities. Magical, humorous, joyful, enlightening, sobering, metaphoric, poetic, life-changing, life-expanding, synchronistic events await you on the other side of that door. One client reported that he experienced such a turnaround with his life that it felt as though he had won the lottery. The prize was a more meaningful, even *remarkable* life.

The secret is to be present in the moment and only in that moment. You are not present when you are talking on your cell phone while standing in the checkout line at the grocery store. In that present moment you might have connected with the person behind you who knew your mother. Or perhaps he might have had led you to the perfect job. You miss out on the amazing communion with the Universe and its messengers when your attention is elsewhere.

The lyrical, hip or transcending music that you listen to on your portable player in the elevator might transport you to some place else. But it is just as likely to take you away from the present moment and all that is going on around you. You might miss the child who looks up at you in that elevator, watching you, ready to connect and make your day. No one brings you back into the present moment like a child or a pet. They know nothing but the present moment.

When we are distracted, we miss the arrival of messengers from the Universe in disguise. Edgar Cayce was the highly intuitive psychic whose readings and teachings have been extensively documented. He recounted a day in the 1940's when he walked into a barbershop. A little boy walked up to him, looked up and said, "Are you still hungry?"

Instantly, Cayce knew that this soul had been one of a group of settlers in another life space. Cayce knew that he, himself, had assisted others in escaping from unfriendly natives in an early American colonial settlement. Many died on a river raft from starvation and exposure. Cayce had been killed by an arrow while making a desperate dash to the riverbank. This child, with no perspective other than the present, was able to speak to Cayce's timeless self.

Overlays such as the experience "remembered" by Edgar Cayce start to "bleed through" into this dimension (see Glossary). You might feel this effect when you meet someone whom you immediately like or dislike or visit a place for the first time and feel oddly at home.

With this type of awareness, you become receptive to images, symbols and other forms of information that arrive through the portal of the present, all which circumvent the linear, rational mind. You become a more integrated soul. As such, you start to recall more aspects of your eternal, evolving identity. You miss all of this when you are not in the present.

Through Which All Blessings Flow

I often interpret for a client's friend or family member who lies in a coma or is afflicted with Alzheimer's. I relay clear, lucid communication from the expanded state of that soul's healthy consciousness, which is undiminished by the state of the body. The dysfunction does not affect the ability of the *soul* to communicate. The information usually rings true for my client.

I also interpret, telepathically, for a client's infant whose consciousness is in no way limited or less knowing because he/she currently inhabits a chronologically young body. Clients often recognize that they too, have experienced similar telepathic communication. But these moments are usually fleeting and unverifiable, making it difficult to trust that this was actually occurring.

It was welcome confirmation for the mother of a son with Down's syndrome when I described a specific moment in the past that I had viewed in her consultation:

"You were walking with your son by some trees with shiny leaves, perhaps magnolias, and you stopped to help him tie his shoe. When you bent over to do so, you looked up at him and your eyes connected. You communicated volumes of understanding to each other. It was as if you had accessed his whole, developmentally '—abled' self."

She smiled, and then acknowledged that she did recall the precise moment that I was accessing. She was able to take note of that moment because she happened to be very present that day as she walked with her son.

It is a true blessing, our ability to communicate with the whole and healthy aspect of others. Another way of describing how it is that we are able to influence and connect in non-physical, non-linear ways is further detailed by Dr. Larry Dossey in his book that I have previously referenced, *Recovering the Soul: A Scientific and Spiritual Search:*

"The main reason to establish the nonlocal nature of the mind is, then, spiritual. Local theories of the mind are not only incomplete, they are destructive. They create the illusion of death and aloneness, altogether local concepts. They foster existential oppression and hopelessness by giving us an utterly false idea of our basic nature, advising us that we are contracted, limited and mortal creatures, locked inside our bodies and drifting inexorably toward the end of time.... If we are nonlocal instead of local creatures, then the world changes for us in the most glorious ways ..."

"Then there is the nature of our relationship to each other. If the mind is nonlocal in space and time, our interaction with each other seems a foregone conclusion. Nonlocal minds are merging minds ... since they are not 'things' that can be walled off and confined to moments in time or point-positions in space."

Your higher consciousness is not partitioned from another's. Regardless of age, distance, disabilities or afflictions, your true and timeless spirit connects you to others on an omnipotent, timeless, higher energetic level.

It transcends your perceptions of differing cultures and beliefs. When you are touched by the plight of war-torn victims and focus heartfelt thoughts and prayers through a corridor of the present, your gifts are received.

You might long to reach out to other peace-loving individuals to share a global vision—one in which diversity of beliefs and cultures is valued and respected. You might yearn for change, derived through honest dialogue and integrity.

Trust that you are uniting through the frequency that connects you to others. When your heart reaches out with focused intention to people in foreign places, you *go* there.

When you imagine conversations with troubled souls in tremendous strife, you *are* with them.

Messages travel from one heart to another, beyond time, distance and death. They can only be censored or doubted by the rational mind. Guided by all that is Divine, this communication of the spirit transmits truth and rejects that which is not authentic.

The Internet is entraining us into a new sense of global connection. I believe that increased awareness of our spirit's intrinsic nature and capabilities is forming a new coalition of humanity. This awareness transcends politics, media-influenced perceptions, external power and greed. It operates beyond all illusion and linear perceptions.

It will become easier for you to recognize participation in multi-sensory transmission once you see how your spirit is in no way confined by physicality, locality or time. As you access your multi-sensory network, you trade in a linear-minded dial-up connection for a "broadband" ability to link up and communicate through the airwaves.

Time, eternal life, our capacity to love and our potential to live fully all exist in the present. It is the portal through which all blessings flow.

Planes and Trains

There have been instances when I was presented with opportunities to respond spontaneously and uninhibited by consensus reality. The freedom and inspiration for me to act in this way was a gift that was delivered to me through the portal of the present. However, I had to *be* in the present to recognize such moments. These occasions most often occurred when I was in a travel mode.

My writer-self tends to be very present. She has the eye to spot the human-interest story in the most mundane situations. Her attention to details encourages me to get to the bottom of things and shape-shift impossible situations into meaningful truths. She even prompts me to make a difference, when I could just as easily run with the herd.

Where travel mishaps would have me playing the victim, my writer-self saves the day. Be it on planes, trains or boats, when she finds me trapped by the unexpected, her observations become ingredients for my writing concoctions.

My inner writer came to the rescue on a lengthy plane flight a few years ago. I was making a three and one-half hour connection from Columbus to Phoenix. Without her watchful eye and love for ironies in life, I surely would have missed an interesting story. Ordinarily, I slip into a light sleep or daydreaming state, the usual effect of numbing plane flights. She elevated me to make something more out of a compromising position.

I was seated between three (count them) crying babies, all on the laps of different parents. A mom and nine-month-old sat in the middle seat, next to mine on the aisle. A not-so-little girl sat in the window seat. Another mom and her year-old son sat in the middle seat in the row before me. A dad and his two-year-old daughter sat cattycorner from me, on the aisle. From where I sat, this arrangement imposed an audial and visual overload.

"*Why me?*" I thought, nearly out loud, before take-off. Then in the same thought-breath, I answered myself, "Why *not* me!" Who could be more sympathetic than a mom who has "been-there-done-that"?

In my mind's eye, I replayed a vignette from over thirty years before. I was flying from California to introduce my first-born six-month-old daughter to meet my grandparents in Boulder, Colorado. With both of my parents deceased, I felt compelled to get the blessings of my grandparents.

That scene featured me perched at the foot of a long flight of stairs in one of the airports. I was immobilized as I stood with my carry-on and baby travel bag at my feet, an umbrella-stroller on one arm and fussy babe in the other. I nearly prayed to get arrested for some infraction, just so that someone might help me carry *something*.

Compassion is defined in the Merriam-Webster Dictionary as "the sympathetic consciousness of others' distress together with a desire to alleviate it." I believe that we can only relate to another from within the context of our own experiences. For example, I could never have interpreted images that I intuited one week before 9/11 in the context of terrorism. It was only after it became part of my own experience that I could interpret such a vision.

Flying with a baby in a crowded plane had certainly had been part of my own past experience. And I was definitely feeling compassion. By mid-flight, the nervous mom next to me was trying everything to keep her baby from whining, crying and disturbing surrounding passengers. Her little girl had already depleted their emergency supply of apple juice. Just before lunch was served, the baby had a diarrhea explosion. Thank God—and I did—that the food carts had not yet pinned us in on both ends of the aisle.

As I pulled myself out into the aisle, I glanced at all the faces looking my way. Instantly, I found myself in a very strategic moment. It seemed as though everyone was assessing my reaction to the situation.

The plane was very still. Already annoyed by the noisy nursery in my sector, the passengers became most attentive. Targeted by their glares, I felt suspended in a distinct and pregnant pause. It was one of those powerful moments when popular consensus is up for grabs. I knew intuitively that I was in a position to influence the reaction of these passengers to the chaos at hand. "So, what is it going to be?" my fellow passengers' glances seemed to say . . .

I flashed to a similar moment when I first moved to New York City. I was jammed in a subway car, my head squeezed into the armpit of a Wall Street commuter. An accident on the Brooklyn Bridge left us stuck on the tracks with all the doors closed. "How shall we take this?" all the passengers seemed to convey by their non-committal expressions. Everyone checked out each other's reactions to the immediate situation.

Taking a deep breath and looking around, I saw a fellow looking directly at me from across the subway car. He smiled, then said, "Aw-righty then, so, uh . . . yer basic cattle drive . . . like, uh, jes' how I wanted to spend *my* afta-noon!"

"Moo!" I yelled back, my head still stuck under my neighbor's arm.

Everyone laughed. The more alert passengers joined in, some snickering, some chortling, but most lightening up in this tight situation. The shift of the energy in the car was unmistakable.

Now on the plane, I found myself in a similar moment, but instead of trying to make light of a tense situation on the tracks, I found myself reaching for a smelly baby with everyone watching. I looked directly across the aisle at the man who was glaring.

"Tough job, bein' a mom!" I said much louder than necessary to be heard across the aisle.

"Uh, er, YES!" answered the man, now smiling very sympathetically and nodding.

I turned to the anxious mom and said, "Here, you hand me the baby, come on out into the aisle, then I'll hand her back to you!" This enabled her to slide out from her tight space. Up and down the aisle, I felt the cabin fill with harmonious and heartfelt compassion. Suddenly, we were all playing for the same team.

Caught in the energy field of others' fears and past perceptions, I might have remained as immobilized and resentful as everyone else around me. Fully present and focused on what was happening, I was able to participate in all that was going on and spontaneously tap into the frequency that connects us. Being fully present even allows us to raise it a few notches.

I trust my inner writer to pull me into the present moment and make it meaningful. Once there, she nudges me to make these entertaining observations and calls upon me to act in consequential ways. Obviously, I took note of what was happening and wrote it down. If not for her, I might have been dozing.

Years ago, an appreciative reader commented about an experience that I shared in *Beyond Boundaries*. I wrote about the frustration I felt at a posh society event. I had a hard time connecting with the guests, most of whom were obsessed with social posturing. I felt peripheral and off-center. I slipped out through the lush gardens and walked to the parking lot. Then I let myself into the back seat of my car, where I chose to disengage and meditate. It was a regenerating and centering gift to myself. I was able to rejoin the gathering, feeling more present and back in my own orbit. I could chat with anyone and maintain a sense of connectedness.

"I never knew we could *do* that!" my reader said. I was shocked but pleased at the notion that reading my story might free her to do something similar in her own life.

When we make choices from observations and insights in the present time, we prompt others to do the same. This is how we make a difference in the world. Remember that the process is contagious. We are all connected telepathically through "streaming" consciousness. Perceiving solely through a linear lens or being everywhere but in the present moment walls us off from each other and blocks the portal through which all blessings flow.

Excursions Outside of Self

It is important to be observant of your life from the perspective of the soul, as if watching yourself in a movie. You begin to sense that there are separate "selves"—one that observes and one that experiences. The observer self has the ability to pull the camera back and reframe scenes that the experiencing self is acting out. While the observer examines the experiencing self in the present moment, it is aware of there being more than just the moment.

As a multi-sensory and multi-dimensional being, you become aware of an ongoing, expansive aspect of your consciousness that is fully operational, regardless of the drama that your ego is playing out. The ability to access higher consciousness positions you to receive "trickle down" insights that often give meaning to the seemingly meaningless in life. It is almost as if you are able to live life in two different "places" at the same time. One level of awareness helps you interpret the other. Life starts to make sense.

Doug is a friend who was in college, living at home with his parents. He fought regularly with his mother. One day, after a horrendous argument, he confided to his friend, Gary, that he didn't think he could live at home any longer. In his characteristically astute manner, Gary said, *"Change her!"*

This prompted Doug to step out of the drama with his mother and observe that their responses were automatic. They were caught in a vicious circle. He realized that if he and his mother were acting out a script, then he could choose to rewrite his lines. The effect of doing so changed the dynamics of their relationship. He had only to break the chain of programmed responses.

Doug stopped losing his temper and started listening to *what* his mother was saying. It was at this point that his observer self realized that it was not what was being said, but *how* it was being said. By calmly expressing his sentiments to his mother, he was able to appeal to her observer-self. This prompted her to change the way she approached him. After that they were able to have a rewarding relationship by concentrating on what they had in common, rather than butting heads by endlessly acting out the controlling-mother, rebellious-son roles.

Included in this important spectrum of self-observation is an ability to pay attention to that which distracts you from being *in* you. Attention to what has momentarily taken you out can become a turn-around moment that actually brings you back *in*.

One of the biggest distracters that take you out of yourself and the present moment is fear. Fear flows in from the past and rises up to distract you from what is actually taking place in the moment. Fears operate like a filter on your viewfinder that skew your perception of the present and influence how you interpret a particular experience. Fears seize control of the present and get projected onto the future. Miss those present moments and you are likely to overlook the gifts that come your way. You will not be able to recognize them.

Some fears rise up from the past. They usually have absolutely nothing to do with what is actually happening in the present. Something in the present may trigger that fear. These triggers are very important to observe. Once observed, you can intentionally program in a new emotional response to an old trigger. For example, you might observe a trigger that prevents you from enjoying a new opportunity when a colleague calls to include you in a new endeavor. He might echo the voice of your overbearing father, unleashing old fears that your efforts will never be good enough. You will not want to even approach the project.

Another trigger might zoom you back to when your teacher berated you, no matter how well you thought you did. Instead of embracing a new opportunity in the present, you might sabotage yourself by procrastinating or running in the opposite direction. Or you might feel resentment toward the one who tried to engage you, rather than appreciating the offer.

Once observed, you can neutralize the effect of fear by acknowledging its presence and allowing yourself to experience the feeling—whatever your child-self felt. After embracing the feeling, release it all to the Source, calling out, "Take this from me and show me what's true!" Then breathe back into the present moment and see what is really going on.

The fastest antidote to overriding fears is shifting to the emotion of gratitude. A grateful heart has no room for fear. I have observed a practical application of this in my work. Loved ones on the Other Side invite clients to visit them in their sleep. They suggest that their last thoughts before drifting off be those of gratitude. Gratitude is a frequency that opens the heart and lets departed loved ones come through more clearly.

Expectations have a similar ability to take you on an excursion out of the present moment.

Suppose you are just about to purchase a lottery ticket. You might find yourself scanning all that you feel your life is lacking. You contemplate all the ways that your winnings will fill that void. In that moment, you are not present.

Once again, gratitude is the best antidote. Spend present moments taking inventory of all that *does* exist in your life for which you can feel grateful. In doing so, you will be present. You will be attentive to what is being delivered. Your feelings of gratitude will attract more into your life and give you cause to feel more gratitude. The gift of the present *is* the present.

Fears

Anything or anyone that you perceive as separate from yourself has power over you. I remember when, as a young girl, my mother would call me into dinner at sundown from playing outside. It was a long walk into the house from our one-half acre of oak trees and grass where we played.

Sometimes I would spook myself by imagining I was being chased by a snake. The faster I walked, the more I was convinced that the snake was going catch me and bite my leg. The more I pretended that the culprit was truly on my heels, the closer it came and the more poisonous and real I believed it to be. By the time I reached the safe zone of my house, I was terrified.

To have simply turned around and embraced the truth about what was—and *wasn't*—an actual threat would have been to neutralize my imagined enemy. When you identify your fears as tangible concerns, they can be dealt with. Sometimes they even dissolve. When you run from fears they become menacing, ominous and bigger than you.

I spent many memorable summers with my grandparents in Boulder, Colorado. In the evenings, we would sit on the front porch and watch people walk by on the sidewalk out front. I recall how Grandmother influenced my impression of the neighbors who lived across the street. She called them "uppity" when they brought home a new car. The old "spinster" down the street "who kept to herself" might as well have been a female version of the fearsome Boo Radley in the bestseller, *To Kill a Mockingbird*.

Bigotry and prejudice stem from this kind of ignorance. They are derived from fearful assumptions regarding those who differ from us in physical characteristics, customs or beliefs. We are often subjected to subtle or even blatant prejudicial beliefs as children.

I personally had no visual images of terrorists from which to stereotype the new ominous enemy before 9/11. I could only relate to my own impressions of menacing movie characters or images of violent rebels, lurking in the jungles of far-away places. My repertoire of experiences included no terrorist references from which to draw conclusions. Visits to my daughter who resides in Israel, combined with the experience of living in Manhattan, both served to alter my image of men from the Middle East dramatically. My previous impression was a stereotypical one of men with harems who live in tents on the desert sand.

It was extremely disheartening after 9/11 to witness the effect of ignorance regarding other cultures that became perceived as "evil" overnight. Too many Americans assumed that anyone with dark hair and darker skin could be presumed to be the enemy. People from India and other foreign countries were attacked and innocent Muslims were condemned. Very soon, in response to the resounding question, *"Why do they hate us?"* Americans received a crucial and expedient education about foreign cultures and beliefs. Many old fears dissolved, while many new ones were fed.

Gathering new information is another powerful way to dissipate fear. Years ago, my two older brothers would often baby-sit my twin brother and me. They would tell us stories to frighten or fool us. They convinced me that the spotlight that streaked through the night sky was a searchlight scanning for escaped convicts. In reality, it was a beacon that announced the opening of a new store.

I also became privy to the truth about those big clicking metal boxes on the side of the highway. My brothers told me that imprisoned dwarves lived inside and were forced to count cars by placing pebbles from one bucket into another with each passing vehicle. I yearned obsessively to release them to freedom. Information gained from maturity dissolved many of my childhood fears.

Most of our fears about the future are created from images fed by consensus reality or pulled from our past repertoire of experiences. Our imagination draws from our conscious experiences and from our unconscious storehouse. Images collected from media, advertising and other modalities influence us subliminally or vicariously. Through a sort of belief osmosis we absorb the collective fears that bombard us as a result of our interaction with society.

New information often neutralizes paranoiac fears. For example, whenever I hold a fear or negative assumption about what I *perceive* that someone is thinking about me, I try, whenever possible, to check out those assumptions by grounding them in reality. Gathering new information is the key.

Over a period of time, two separate friends moved out of my life after hurting me deeply. I could not understand what I had done to cause them to dislike me. Obsessive speculation drove me crazy. I happened to meet up with them at different times, years later, through synchronistic events. I mustered the courage to ask each of them what I had done to deserve their unkindness.

I was shocked when they confessed that their actions in the past came from feelings of jealously toward me. Whenever the effects of that particular emotion hit me, I find them to be the most perplexing to decipher. I am astounded to discover the origin of that type of unkindness, wondering what another might have found in me about which to feel such jealousy.

I suspect that my bewilderment came more from my inability to stand in their shoes than from self-effacing humility. All that time I was certain that those past friends had learned something dark about me that I had yet to discover and fix through my own process of self-discovery. Actually, I have to admit that there might have been some truth to this. The more confidence I have gained through the years, the more inclusive I am able to be with others.

Jealously and envy seldom rear their heads when the spotlight is shared with others. These days, nothing makes me happier than to shine the spotlight on my apprentices as they progress in becoming effective "receivers."

Things are never as they seem. Checking out assumptions and finding them to be erroneous can be extremely empowering, as well as liberating. Ninety-nine percent of the time, that which you fear that others are thinking about you is *simply not accurate*. Most often, you are projecting the fears and insecurities that you have about yourself onto others. Additionally, you might be quite surprised to discover the misguided assumptions that others might be holding regarding what *they* think you feel about *them*.

Carrying my own assumptions about the friends who hurt me caused me to hold onto misguided fears. Worrying that others might know more of my "dark side" than I might know or discover about myself would have been an unfortunate burden. I would have lived with growing self-scorn and increasing distrust of myself and for others.

There was an unpleasant period in my career when I was attracting a certain element of people. They were extremely cruel and condemning of me because of fear-based religious beliefs that taught them that people like myself were "doing the work of the devil." These "true believers" treated me with more unkindness than I have yet to experience in my entire life. More than once, they intruded and interrupted private conversations, regardless of the time or place.

When I moved my children to a new location in the Bay Area of California following my divorce, there was a woman who lived in our condominium complex who was the wife of the president of the homeowner's association. She traveled up and down Main Street to warn shopkeepers about the evil woman who had come to town. The "righteous" would also call in to interrupt radio interviews with their venomous condemnations. Over time, I became desensitized to these attacks and barely noticed their intrusive accusations.

On one occasion, a radio host became more upset than I ever did when a listener called in to warn me of my transgressions. Her condemnations were pretty predictable.

"Excuse me!" the host interrupted the caller. "Am I to assume that you have accepted Jesus Christ as your personal Savior?"

"Oh, yes! That is very true!" the woman replied, enthusiastically.

"And therefore, am I to assume that you believe that Jesus Christ taught others to love and accept one another?"

"Uh, yes, that is also true," she responded.

"Well then, what I want to know is, where is the love? You call in, viciously condemning and judging Ms. Hauck. . . . *Where . . . is . . . the . . . love . . . and . . . acceptance?*"

When the caller hung up, the host asked me over the air, "And now, Ms. Hauck, what are your feelings about this?" My response had become pretty standard by that time:

"We all come from different influences and perspectives. I would never impose my way of seeing things on another. Nor will I allow another to impose upon me that which does not resonate with my truth. That said, fear and love cannot coexist."

These people finally stopped showing up in my life. In retrospect, I have gained insights as to why I might have been attracting them in the first place. Long ago I learned that what we experience in our physical world is a reflection of our own thoughts, fears and beliefs, which are mirrored back to us through the events and people that we attract into our lives.

Therefore, I have concluded that these God-fearing and fearsome people must have actually represented a reflection of my own hesitation about doing this work. When I was finally and absolutely convinced that my work is divinely inspired and Divinely blessed, those people disappeared from my life.

Whenever they do make the occasional reappearance in my life, I try to narrow my separating perceptions by exploring that which might connect us, looking for some commonality in our differing beliefs. Sometimes I make myself listen to fundamentalist radio broadcasts when I drive around cities where I have speaking engagements. I make the effort to listen to what they are trying to say, even when I do not understand them or agree with them.

Occasionally, I find some little overlap with my own perceptions. The challenge for me is to try not to emphasize all that divides us, but to find that which connects us. Then there can be love and maybe even some respect, instead of fear.

Being among those who are led to explore the unknown, I can observe how certain fears about psychic phenomena are quelled when new information is collected. Just think of the fearful impressions that are altered when audiences watch people like me demonstrate communication with the dead. Fears about haunting ghosts and tormented souls fall away. Communication from loved ones confirms that they are at peace and have never stopped loving us.

I laugh when I think about something that a friend said to me over dinner one evening, after I described someone as being "pretty eccentric." My friend leaned over the table where we sat in the restaurant and whispered, "Louise, may I remind you that you are one who 'talks to dead people?'" I laughed, thinking of how different perceptions create different realities. I mused at how drastically our views can change, depending upon our vantage point.

Embracing whatever you perceive as separate from yourself will counteract the unfounded fears, which are notorious for taking you out of the beam of Divine Light. Gaining new understanding about those who do not view life in the same way will open you to the joys and adventures of exploring diversity in the world. Your life expands and your connection to others—and to the Source—grows deeper. And the world becomes a safer place.

FOUR

The Presence of the Past

*"The door to the
soul opens in."*

—Eric Butterworth

Through the portal of the present I enter into a "no-time zone" where past, present and future coexist. When I merge with a client's timeless consciousness, I can experience his or her childhood as if I am there. It is not so much that I go back in time; rather, I can access it because it is happening now.

Seeing through my client's eyes, we might be hiding, crouched under the stairs, along with tennis rackets and a vacuum cleaner. We might be in a dark closet where I can smell the scent of old shoes and mothballs. We might find ourselves sharing the cramped space with an ironing board or Mom's off-season dresses hanging around my head. Sometimes, I am under beds, along with dust bunnies and gift-wrapping supplies. I can hear the yelling of a drunken father, the arguing of frustrated parents, the chiding of an older sibling or the approach of a menacing relative.

I recall asking a client, "What is this about your father, wielding a knife? Was your father a butcher?"

"No," she replied, emotionless. "When my father was drunk, he would come at us with a butcher knife."

"Yikes!" I thought to myself. I often have difficulty identifying and interpreting events that have not been part of my own experience.

"Now I'm feeling that we're being locked in a closet," I continued with my client.

"My stepbrothers used to lock me in the closet where a previous occupant had been murdered," she replied, calmly.

By contrast, I often find my clients' child-selves retreating to a safe oasis. We might be sitting in a grandmother's living room near the end table that holds a crystal dish with butterscotch candy. We might be looking down from a secret tree house, watching the father drive into the garage after work or hearing the voice of the mother calling my client to lunch.

Sometimes I experience the delight of a secret, backyard cave, carved out of dense shrubbery. Cigar boxes and cookie tins safeguard precious items from nosy siblings or neighborhood bullies. Storm drains and rural gullies conceal us from those who might intrude or abuse in physical, emotional or sexual ways.

From that vantage point, merged with my client's consciousness, I access false beliefs that were forming. For example, many clients learned to believe that they were unlovable or undeserving. These types of beliefs can set in motion decades of repeating negative patterns.

Sometimes old patterns go back beyond this lifetime. Co-existing overlays in other life spaces confirm this. Repeating themes appear as though they are stacked directly on top of present life scenarios. The similarities can be amazing.

In many instances, personal beliefs become self-fulfilling prophecies. Enlightenment is hastened by taking note of negative perceptions carried into adulthood. In a metaphysical context, like attracts like. Perceptions of being unlovable, undeserving or untrustworthy tend to attract situations that reflect back those negative qualities. Landlords, overbearing employers, parent figures, bossy neighbors or dominating spouses respond accordingly to our beliefs about ourselves.

Utilizing this ability to retrieve and change the past, I reposition the child-self to receive validation, unconditional love and encouragement. An alternate reality is then created, one in which that child is learning to honor his or her truth. Greater self-trust is sent through the corridor from the past to my client in the present.

Once I have explored the past, I move forward through time, giving examples of repeating patterns. Then I follow a thread to the most positive potential shift in the future. There, I uncover a specific moment and describe details being experienced by my client. I scan for perceptions that contrast with those in the past. I explore all that is new and different. Sometimes I can find out more about my clients in the present by accessing their future memories!

Adopting the Child

After viewing horrific verbal abuse in Fran's childhood, I was prompted to begin her session by working with her little girl-self.

First, we successfully opened up the corridor from the present to the past. Then, I pulled a thread to a positive future moment. This moment was likely to manifest if she were able to embrace and nurture the little girl she left behind. That child-self was eager to send forth precious gifts of creativity, spontaneity and playfulness. Her diary was full of memories to send through flashbacks and dreams. Receiving and integrating these gifts in the present could transform Fran's future.

I described to Fran a sample of what she was feeling in that possible future. She said, "You say 'feelings' . . . and I just feel confused." Just the *thought* of feeling something was extremely confusing to her. Feelings can be so painful that some children become disassociated from them. As adults, they are left with an inability to relate to any feelings.

I witness dramatic evidence that this procedure of opening corridors beyond time is actually happening. Our child-selves really do co-exist in the present. This concept is clearly illustrated in the following account.

I consulted for Gail, who was wrestling with many health problems, including obesity. After addressing some of these issues, I merged with her childhood consciousness. She was three years old. Her grandfather had just left her bedroom, shutting the door quietly behind him. He was sexually molesting her on a regular basis.

Gail could not remember anything from her painful past. Merging with her timeless consciousness, it was if I were sitting on her bed, looking around her bedroom for props that might trigger a memory. Clients need to relate to *something* in the past in order to open a corridor.

Gail could not recall owning a "magic rock garden," a majorette baton or the iridescent abalone shell that I viewed on a bookshelf. Finally, I mentioned the Charlie McCarthy ventrilo-quist doll, which I spotted sitting in the corner. That suddenly triggered a memory. She remembered it with delight.

"We're in!" I exclaimed, sensing that we had just success-fully brought her through the corridor from the present to her concurrent past. Once Gail could feel or see herself there in her bedroom, I encouraged her to invite that little girl to come from her unsafe past and join up with my client in a safe adulthood.

"PSSST! I'm over here," were the thoughts that I encour-aged Gail to send, telepathically, to the little girl in the past. Merging with the girl's consciousness as she sat in her bedroom, I could see her watching a sphere of light opening up, like the aperture of a camera. It revealed the face of her future self.

"It's safe to come join me now, in your future," I continued to prompt my client in the present to relay to herself in the past. "You can come live with me now! I will keep you safe, love you unconditionally and give you my undivided attention! I can sup-port you in expressing yourself fully and in becoming all that you are here to be!"

Sometimes this exercise brings tears to my clients' eyes. The child-self in the past feels loved like never before. At this point in the process, Gail interrupted me.

"Wait a sec!" she exclaimed. "I just remembered. When I was three years old, *I heard a voice saying these very words to me!* They got me through. I held onto them for years."

"Hol-y mol-y," I thought to myself, realizing the power of working beyond time. "This is really happening." To think that thirty years before that day in 1998, Gail's little girl-self heard us talking to her.

I did a similar corridor-opening exercise with another client and her child-self. At the end of the session she said, "You know, it's really funny. When I was a little girl, I knew that someday my future self would be talking to me. I didn't know what that meant. It just happened."

Helen is a woman in her early thirties who was an apprentice. We were working together weekly, over the phone. I was focusing on positioning her to be a more effective receiver. We were talking when I suddenly felt Helen block her reception of intuitive information. Her little girl-self came to me from her past. She felt extremely present and interactive. The little girl was sitting in the front row of her fourth grade class, wearing a plaid jumper. I described this to the apprentice.

"Oh, that was the school uniform that I wore in Catholic school. I remember that class. The nun had favorite students. She constantly made me feel excluded and wrong whenever I responded to her questions. I learned to never raise my hand."

Not only was the little girl ready to be validated and repositioned, but she also wanted to send a gift to her future self—to Helen in the present. From the past, the little girl sent me the name "Rose" and a scene of herself, sitting by a houseplant in someone's kitchen. I described the scene to my apprentice.

"Gosh!" Helen exclaimed. "I can't believe how all of this relates to something that just happened last weekend. My mother and I never got along. She always made me feel stupid. She used to *call* me 'stupid!' Lately, I've been trying to be stronger when Mom criticizes me and not just stand there and take it like a shamed child.

"So that's exactly what I did last weekend," Helen continued. "My mother and I were having an argument. It actually involved her old friend, Rose. I disagreed with something Mom said, and she tossed her iced tea down the front of my blouse. I told her that I would no longer take that from her and I left."

Then Helen mentioned an incident that took place when she was in grade school, around the same time that she was in the nun's fourth grade class. "We were visiting Mom's friend, Rose. We were standing in her kitchen one day," she began. "Mom and Rose were talking. I reached over to pluck off a few dead leaves from Rose's plants. I'd heard that it promoted growth. Mother screamed at me. She embarrassed me terribly." Helen's little girl-self was attempting to communicate her need for validation by sending a reminder of the incident.

To validate the past is not to cast aspersions or blame others. Rather, it is saying, "Yes! That did happen. It felt awful. I can trust what I feel. That is my truth. I can feel safe now, trusting what I feel in the present."

I also find that child-selves send specific gifts from the past to the present self. When I receive notice of an upcoming "delivery" of such a gift, I alert the client to be on the lookout (but not obsessively) for certain objects that are soon to appear on their periphery. These gifts can manifest while window shopping or strolling around town. The "gift" is usually a toy or object that is reminiscent of a client's childhood. It could be a set of jacks, a pinwheel, model airplane, deck of cards or a picture. At such an occurrence, I encourage the client to purchase the object and place it on a small altar on which to honor the child in the past.

Similarly, deceased loved ones send gifts between dimensions, sometimes through wildlife. The bird or butterfly that comes to perch on your windowsill can be the sign you have prayed for. Other gifts will surprise you in how they arrive. A client was amazed to find a brilliantly colored black and red dragonfly land on the plant by her front door the day after her favorite aunt's memorial service. The insect wore the aunt's favorite color combination. Her aunt confirmed this in a consultation.

Ingrid lost her husband, leaving her to raise their little girl alone. Whenever they find a penny on the ground, she reminds her daughter that it was sent from her Daddy, from heaven. He had said that he would do that, on his deathbed.

Consciousness truly exists in all of time. Adopting and nurturing the child-self shifts perceptions. It heals and transforms the past issues that create stumbling blocks in the present. An entirely new and positive future becomes available when the past is changed.

Occupying the Premises

Some people have an awareness that *something* continues to sabotage their personal and professional lives . . . something that is hard to define. It comes from an inability to maintain a focus in the present moment. I find this to be a constant challenge in the lives of many of my clients. They have heard a variety of feedback from family, friends and colleagues, such as, "You're not with me," "You go somewhere else," "You must not be interested," "I'm unable to share special moments with you," or "It takes too much energy to be with you."

They realize that there is a gremlin afoot, a stumbling block that gets in the way of more intimate relationships. We are all being challenged in these times to maintain a greater focus in the midst of countless distractions. High-pitched news reports, technological conveniences—including the use and maintenance thereof—devour our attention. Multi-tasking spirals us into an ever-increasing disassociation from what is actually happening right now.

When the gremlin of distraction rears its head, it diverts us and causes us to vacate the present. It is as if we are no longer on the planet. But sometimes the gremlin has a more serious origin than mundane distractions. It is one that the child-self is anxious to address. This is when going beyond time can be extremely helpful.

Children who grow up amidst abuse, alcoholism or chaos are often conditioned to live in a hyper-vigilant state. This shapes them to become extremely attentive and perceptive (in some cases, obsessive) to all that is going on around them. In adulthood, they live with an ongoing challenge to find their way to a deeper place within themselves. They struggle to define personal boundaries. This journey of self-discovery can lead them to greater self-trust and more meaningful relationships.

I was standing before a large audience, about to begin the "tuning-in" segment of my presentation. The usual telepathic plea from audience participants came through quite clearly—"Do me! Do me!" Ignoring them, I focused on a woman in the front row.

"I see that you were recently doing something with a number of young girls," I began, starting to tune in.

"No . . ." she replied, shaking her head.

"Yes, you were!" exclaimed a man at the back of the room. "You ran the Girl Scout Jamboree last weekend." The woman was surprised to discover that a co-worker from her office was attending.

"Oh, yeah . . ." the woman confirmed, looking somewhat bewildered.

I sensed that this woman was unable to be present. I pulled a thread to her past and experienced a moment in her childhood when she was around five or six years old. Her parents were yelling and screaming at each other. At the same time, they were berating their little girl—this woman's child-self—as well as her siblings. She recognized nothing that I reported from the past.

"You used to love red licorice." I said, attempting to open the corridor to where her little girl-self desperately needed her validation and love.

"I don't know . . . I don't remember . . ." she replied.

"Do you like red licorice *now?*" I asked.

"I don't . . . know . . ." she said, frowning.

The woman was unable to remember anything from her childhood. She had completely disassociated from painful feelings in the past and from feelings in general. As a result, she did not know what she felt about anything in the present. She had grown up learning that to be present—to feel *feelings*—was neither a safe nor a pleasant place to be.

A residual effect from this type of disassociation in the present is an inability to be decisive. If you don't know what you feel, how are you going to know what you prefer or what to choose about anything in your life?

Ingrid is a high-powered legislator in Washington, DC. She operates solely from her brilliant, logical mind. Consultations with analytical, "mental" clients are usually the most challenging. These clients are unable to comprehend abstract symbols and interpret metaphors. They overemphasize the concrete and literal, interpreting information through logic.

Ingrid's little girl-self was desperately trying to warn her about a repeating theme that involved choosing abusive men. She had much to share with her future self. I intuitively retrieved a list of boys and men from the past who typified my client's dysfunctional relationships. To become aware of this trend might have allowed transformation and open Ingrid to new and healthier associations in the near future. She could not understand what in the world I was talking about.

"The past is the past. That where it's best to leave it—in the past!" she exclaimed. Ingrid seemed quite defensive regarding her inability to remember much of the past. "What does 'my little girl-self' have to do with this? I want you to tell me about a new man in my life."

Seduction, Martyrdom and Manipulation

Years ago, I returned an article of clothing to a department store. The salesperson at the counter reached for a return form and asked, bluntly, "Reason for return?"

I looked at her and replied, "I don't need it."

She looked at the form, commenting, "There's no box to check for that." Two other salespeople sashayed over to see what was going on. I thought they were going to come unglued. The truth is often found outside the box.

When you speak your truth in all moments, you transmit a very strong signal. Truth and authenticity oscillate at a high frequency. At this elevated frequency, your vibration reaches others and gives them permission to speak *their* truth. It's contagious!

Historically, women have not been supported in communicating what is on their minds. Suppressed emotions become articulated in subversive or passive-aggressive ways, such as gossip, manipulation and deception. I personally believe that gossip is backwash from truths not spoken.

I observe that when many women clients become more self-realized, they gain greater self-trust. They become more focused in their intentions and actions. They are able to speak up in more direct and honest ways. When operating in a present and conscious way, clear and concise words come easier. There is less unfinished business to regurgitate at a later time. All is said and done in the present.

It came to me in meditation one day that as women are evolving and adopting more truthful communication, they are disabling three ancient survival mechanisms: seduction, martyrdom and manipulation. Many women from the "baby boomer" generation, like myself, learned at least two out of three of those tactics from our mothers. Martyrdom was probably at the top of the list. Speaking truth that flows from higher guidance allows such maneuvers to fall away.

Telling the truth in all moments creates a momentum that carries you over the shortest route. To maneuver against this momentum feels like a tedious detour. Once in this force of truth, your spirit simply cannot flow in any other direction.

My mother had her own martyrdom routine. I have an indelible image of her injured look when she suffered silently, just as her mother (and her mother's mother) had been raised to do. My brothers and I often felt as though we were walking on eggshells. When my twin brother married, he told his bride, "If you *ever* give me *that look*, the marriage is over!" (They have a wonderful and lasting marriage.)

Had my mother been able to share her frustrations with me, it would have been an invaluable gift. I might have more tolerance for my own frustrations. I would have also gained tools from watching my parents resolve issues more openly. I might have received a jump-start in communicating more directly with people. I might have also become more forgiving and less apologetic for my own human frailties, frustrations and imperfections, had I been allowed to observe those very real qualities in my parents. Their generation was more concerned with matching the illusion of the "Ozzie and Harriet" family. There were elephants residing in many living rooms in those days, free to roam without the truth being addressed.

To awaken spiritually is to live more in the moment, and that has a remarkable effect. The human spirit is liberated. A freed spirit is no longer constricted by fear. It can then emanate a vitality that is fortifying and life-affirming. Living fearlessly allows the spirit to flow in its truest form—with truth and authenticity. It steers the soul away from manipulation or deception. It becomes easier to speak truth.

Emotions are energy, as is everything in life. When not expressed, aired and allowed to transform, energy can stagnate and can become cancerous. I can only wonder if greater self-expression might have also spared my mother the agonizing pain of breast cancer that she suffered before passing at the age of fifty-one. I never saw her grieve openly after the passing of my father when he died of colon cancer, also at the age of fifty-one. There are few rewards for martyrdom.

Seduction is a maneuver that has also served as a survival mechanism in our patriarchal world. Women have seduced soldiers to procure food to feed the village or to save their own lives and those of their children. Women often seduce, consciously and unconsciously, to gain power in unsafe or uncertain moments. I also observe male clients who do the same in order to control women when they are feeling insecure.

When I sense that I am consulting for a very seductive client, I suggest the following exercise: Observe your next encounter when a sexual impulse is triggered. It does not matter who initiates it. Resist the impulse. Let it go by. Watch it . . . They report very revealing observations.

Clients report that their first revelation is a surprising one: their compulsion is to seduce or manipulate when new circumstances present themselves. New situations often trigger a fear of the unexpected, the future or the unknown. They may bring up fears from the past tied to rejection and abandonment. The ego-self will do whatever it can to protect against that kind of grief or uncertainty. Seduction is a reflexive response, which temporarily suspends those fears and replaces them with the feeling of being in charge.

The second revelation that they report: the impulse to seduce often inhibits insights that could enlighten them as to the purpose of meeting a certain person in the first place. Sometimes the soul is simply recognizing an old friend, but the ego-self misinterprets, "Wow! He/she must be *the one.*" There are always gifts to receive in any type of relationship, but the gift is lost when seduction eclipses these observations.

Jeanne felt this way about a man she had recently met, convinced that he must be her soul mate. "He's married and has five children," she added sheepishly, as she told me the story. "But I just *know* that he is my soul mate."

"Why do you think that your paths are configured to make you unavailable to each other in this lifetime? I asked. "Chances are that you've 'been there ... done that,' having experienced a similar role in another life space. It is likely that you are misinterpreting that feeling of soul familiarity. Most likely, you are reuniting to play a new role, to support something new in each other."

Sure enough, in Jeanne's consultation we discovered that the two of them had owned a general store together in a prairie lifetime (or more accurately, in another "life space"). In that scenario, Jeanne was playing the role of a supportive but extremely submissive wife. She lived that life without the opportunity to discover and explore her own creativity and ingenuity.

We then understood that the soul currently playing the character of this attractive, married man had been written into Jeanne's script so that he might return the favor in this time around. He was compelled to support her emerging spiritual and creative awakening.

In another instance, I offered the seduction observation exercise to Karen, a successful model. Her seductive manner came through very clearly, even over the phone. At the time, she was going through the latest of several divorces. A few months later, she notified me of the results of her deliberate observations.

Karen reported, "I actually did notice the next time that I felt the urge to seduce. It came up when I met with my divorce lawyer. We were sitting at my dining room table. The feeling just came over me. It was powerful."

She went on to describe how she allowed the feeling to pass. She said that by simply observing and not acting on that impulse, she was able to allow her lawyer to do his job much more effectively. They become good friends.

Years ago, I was collaborating with an Episcopal priest in conducting a workshop. I was going through my own divorce at the time, feeling quite vulnerable. Apparently, I was being seductive. The priest mentioned that it was "very flattering" to work with me. I did not understand what he was implying. As we discussed it further, I confessed to him—pun intended— my penchant for a certain theme in old movies. I loved it when actresses, such as Audrey Hepburn, played the part of the woman who was determined and successful in seducing the priest out of his vows. I thought it was very sexy.

The priest's response was extremely enlightening. "That is *so* symbolic! I would surmise that you are currently on a search for your 'animus,'" he proclaimed, referring to my imminent need to discover and integrate my own male aspects.

It was time for me to become more proactive and assertive. It was also time for me to embrace that kind of courage and get over my old, flirtatious, people-pleasing tendencies. The soul is neither male nor female, and embodies aspects of both. My male within me was prepared to come to my rescue.

At the same time, I was gaining greater trust in my powerful, feminine, intuitive and nurturing qualities. To incorporate more male aspects and balance them with my powerful female energy would prove to be a dynamic combination.

The priest also felt that I was seeking my ultimate God-self. In our civilization, we have been taught that God is patriarchal. God is a "He." The priest surmised that I was projecting this search—for my ultimate (male) God-self—onto men. I was seeking my truth and strength from the first man who might turn my head.

I later discovered that I also had some forgiveness to work out from experiences with the Church during other life spaces. To seduce the priest was to get even. Given this unconscious symbolic agenda, no wonder those possibilities felt so compelling.

In the following and extremely challenging months, I was pulled through my own personal "dark night of the soul." I was forced to surrender to a Higher Power for strength and guidance. I had no choice but to reach into my depths for courage and embrace the insights from resulting epiphanies.

I emerged from that period of my life grateful to be empowered, having embraced more of my own "macho" aspects. To my amusement, I noticed that I no longer enjoyed the type of movies that featured a tough, sexy guy, such as Clint Eastwood or Charles Bronson, where he grabs the innocent, helpless damsel and forcefully throws her into the hay with an imposing, "Come 'ere, girl!"

Surprisingly, in my own life, I noticed that I no longer fantasized about a man who might dominate me. Gone was the illusion that he who is male might deliver my truth. My life's challenges were forcing me to discover my own.

Past Life Overlays Affecting Different Futures

In the way that you can reposition yourself in your childhood by opening a corridor from the present to the past, you can do the same by traveling from the present through a corridor to previous life spaces. In consultations, I find it the most helpful to look at past life experiences metaphorically.

Unresolved issues or false beliefs that restricted the soul's journey in past life spaces resurface and become amplified for the purpose of healing and transformation. Unfinished business often presents itself, compelling the soul to continue on—pretty much from where it left off—and proceed towards resolution. These can be troublesome or unexplainable issues that arise, the origins of which are difficult to trace.

It is as if past selves send forth the opportunity to play out an old drama on today's stage. In the way that there exists an eternal continuum of consciousness, a sort of sequel is set in motion, configured in a way to prompt the reading of a new script and the discovery of new truths.

Hypnotherapy, past life regressions and guided meditations are helpful in uncovering original scenarios. Past fears and unfinished business show up and their relevance to present issues is revealed. Once resolved and integrated, that past self can metaphorically die in peace. The present self then moves forward, toting a lighter bag.

It is my perception that there are particular life spaces from which we have exited with certain distorted beliefs. There may have been deathbed reflections that convinced you of your unworthiness, sometimes due to condemnation, betrayal or abandonment. In the course of your soul's journey, once again you are presented with the gift of life, another opportunity to seek truth. Childhood circumstances set the stage and serve as a springboard for new, expanding and freeing realizations.

In the way that your child-self sends gifts, so do past selves, from other life spaces. They hold aspects of your timeless essence which are still accessible. Gifts might include untapped talents or skills, creative potentials and courage. For example, I discovered that I am my own grandmother. It is more accurate to say that I carry an aspect of my father's mother. My parents named me after his mother, Louise Platt Hauck. She died in 1943 and I was born in 1946. I am not that same personality, but instead, carry forth a measure of that particular energy pattern.

I have heard it said that we do not reincarnate for at least four hundred years. That does not make sense to me, since there is no timeframe in the dimension from which we re-enter. Some feel that when a soul returns in quick succession, it is either very drawn to this physical dimension or it returns on a specific mission. I would imagine that the second possibility is truer in my case. I have found it to be a matter of the most ideal configuration that draws a soul back into this dimension, rather than reincarnation being a time-related matter.

Conditions favorable for re-entry might involve a group of souls who come to participate in the spiritual awakening of others, sometimes at a strategic time in history. Some souls assist in bringing heaven to Earth by showing all that man can be on the Earth. The souls who were born to bravely make their exit in the 9/11 tragedy and the family members they left behind might serve as an examples of both these conditions.

My grandmother/myself was a writer who authored eighty books and three hundred short stories. Over the years, more than one client has sent me one of her books found in an old used bookstore or yard sale. "Are you related?" is the usual enclosed message.

Louise Platt Hauck was also a historian for the Pony Express in St. Joseph, Missouri. One of her novels, *The Youngest Rider*, details the life of one of its messengers. Her passion for writing found her at a time when she was reading all day and writing into the night. She supported three families through the Great Depression with the revenue from her published books and articles. She began taking sleeping pills for much-needed rest, a habit that eventually necessitated a short stay in a sanitarium.

In my current life space, my first job was in a hospital for the mentally disabled where I worked as a music therapist in research. Later, I worked with developmentally disabled children as a behavior modification specialist. If I consider the path of my soul's journey chronologically, I might speculate that events in this life positioned me to ask, "Let's see, where did I leave off?"

I lived for three years at the foot of the Colorado Rockies, the same mountains to where my former self traveled from Missouri to spend every possible summer in a family mountain cabin. A life-long desire to explore that area confirmed a "bleedthrough" effect into this life space. After three years there, my life's plan moved me on.

While living in Colorado, one summer evening I received a clear and unmistakable revelation that shifted my reality. I was given my next "marching orders." The vision came to me in the middle of a movie that I was watching in a theater. Within three weeks, I had sold everything and arrived at my next destination, New York City.

It amuses me to contemplate that in this life space, I got along so much better with my mother, as her daughter, than I did as her mother-in-law. A faint soul memory from that life space sometimes flashes recognition of my (then) daughter-in-law's spiritual radiance, a quality that was a bit intimidating. My mother was known for being an extraordinarily inspiring and talented woman. As her mother-in-law, I sought to understand her kind of illumination. Inevitably, reincarnating as her daughter made that possible.

I was blessed to have come to a mother who supported my early spiritual visions and intuitions. When I was four years old, I said to her, "When you go to heaven, we'll write letters!" This was a precognitive sensing that I would eventually be in communication with souls on the Other Side. My mother smiled and nodded, supporting my internal knowing. Her passing was the catalyst for my spiritual awakening.

Trusting that I carry certain aspects of that other "Louise" helps me understand and explore a persistent curiosity involving the craft of writing. It also helps me understand intermittent fears that sometimes surface regarding the writing process. The intensity of the creative process could swallow me up if I fail to make the effort to live a balanced life.

A variety of aspects in past selves can influence your present reality. An excellent example was demonstrated during a consultation with Lois, a woman in her mid-forties:

"Can you bring my grandmother here?" she asked. "She died before I was born. All my life, I have been obsessively curious out about her!"

"She's right here," I said, merging with her grandmother's timeless consciousness. "I am experiencing her standing in the kitchen on the farm, looking out the window. There is an ache in her heart about 'the one who left home' at an early age."

"That would be my father," Lois replied.

"A very boorish man just stomped into the kitchen," I continued.

"That's probably my abusive grandfather. He was very mean when he drank," she confirmed.

"Your grandmother is feeling quite miserable. She does not know how to get out of this unbearable living situation," I said.

"She committed suicide," she replied.

At that precise moment, I saw a thread that extended from the grandmother, existing beyond time, to Lois who sat before me in the present.

"You were that grandmother!" I exclaimed. Then I detailed how it was more accurate to state that Lois carried a major aspect of that energy projected as her grandmother.

I saw that the soul now known as Lois was once again unhappily married in an unfulfilling and joyless life. I also saw that she currently worked with people in some counseling capacity.

"I'm a grief counselor," she confirmed.

"How absolutely poetic," I exclaimed. There she was, once again having been given the gift of life in which to evolve. This time, Lois worked in an occupation in which it was her duty to sit and observe the tormenting effect of losing a loved one— precisely what she caused others to experience when she made the choice to end her life in that other life space. Any attempt to judge, exact punishment or determine consequences for others' misdeeds pales in comparison to the creative and balancing design of the Universe.

As we evolve to a more awakened state, we become more integrated souls by remembering aspects of our timeless selves. It is important to remain detached from past personalities we have adopted in order to explore the physical dimension. There is a temptation to become infatuated with past adventures, particularly when current experiences feel mundane or boring.

People who have been told by psychics that they were a famous person are sometimes receiving little more than a bit of "ego-fluffing." Sometimes, however, the information resonates, especially when confirmed by actual, experienced "bleedthroughs" (see Glossary). However, it would be more accurate to say that the person "carries an aspect" of the energetic representation of that person of historical acclaim, rather than to claim that he was that person.

I once wrote: "There are those who are enchanted to find that they are from another planet. They announce this, as if their intention is to disclaim, 'I'm not really *from* here,' thereby giving them permission to circumvent issues that challenge them in the present. If, instead, they focus on their issues, they are sure to receive gifts that will be welcome in *any* galaxy."

Along with being in the here and now, it is helpful to be aware of your ongoing timeless aspects, to trust your potentials and overcome old fears. In this lifetime you have the opportunity to expand and become greater than any self you have ever played.

FIVE

Accessing the future

*"The present is pregnant
with the future."*

—Voltaire

Sometimes people think that because I can see their future, I created it. I remember describing a future partner to a client. I was doing this in the context of pointing out an old, repeating pattern to which I felt she needed to pay attention. I explained that if she should choose to observe her tendency to play the victim in relationships, there was a good chance that this pattern could change. Such a transformation would position her to meet this new partner, who differed dramatically from the men in her past. I described him as I saw him, existing in a probable future. She pondered my counsel, then asked, "Can't you see him a little taller?"

I get a very itchy feeling when people give me such power. It is not mine, and I do not desire it. The moment that clients relinquish their own personal power, I feel a tremendous energy drain. They toss it into my lap with statements such as, "So, you *do* think, then, that I'll be happily married?" or "So, my kids *will* be okay, then?" I start to yawn and become very sleepy.

Conversely, I experience quite the opposite effect when I consult for awakened clients who have learned how to surrender to a Higher Power. They know when the Universe is directing them to move on a decision full-throttle and when a barricade simply represents a free-will choice that is going nowhere. They have learned how to ask for guidance *before* life lets them down, requesting clear and gentle road signs. I am impressed with their growing ability to identify and interpret the answers they receive.

When I consult for these clients, we can truly get their consultation off the ground. The experience is fun and enlightening for everyone involved. I upload clairvoyant images of past, present and probable futures; communication from the client's timeless, all-knowing, Higher Self; and messages from transitioning (coming in, going out and departed) souls. After I take a moment to sort it all out, I download all the images and information. The client and I then proceed together in a delightful duet, interpreting entertaining charades, meaningful metaphors and humorous puns.

"I see you sliding into the next chapter, on a road that looks as smooth as cake icing."

"Yes! I hope to return to my life's passion—cake decorating," chimes the client.

"You're coming out of a period that looks as if you were skipping along, then tripped over a pothole and turned back around to beat it to death with your shoe," I say to another.

"You're referring to my time in Scranton, Pennsylvania. It's known as 'the pothole of the Universe.' Let's just say that after I moved there, I stayed too long. Nothing went well. I finally moved away . . . and I am second only to Imelda Marcos when it comes to collecting shoes."

"Your father [on the Other Side] is doing a pantomime. It is as if he's shaking a money tree with silver dollars hanging from the branches . . ."

"Our last name is 'Money.' My sister recently mentioned Dad's silver dollar collection that she found in her basement. He saved them from the Korean War. He must want us to sell them for some extra money."

What a refreshing contrast from days when some clients would sit with arms folded across the chest, unable (or unwilling) to help me decipher the images during the downloading phase of a consultation. "You tell *me!*" one client barked, when I asked if there was a "Chris" in the family. I was picking up on her son, with whom she had several issues to resolve.

"What do you want from me?" I thought, feeling extreme frustration. I continued to interpret additional information onto the client's tape, reminding her to *please* listen to it at a future date. I hoped that at such a time her heart might be receptive. During the session, her analytical mind stood in the way of a potentially validating experience.

Some clients simply seek confirmation of their own interpretation of door-opening *synchronicities*—no longer referred to as *coincidences*. They receive assurances that their personal paths are unfolding in the highest and most flowing way. We all need assistance in navigating from time to time, whether it comes from an intuitive source or through more traditional forms of counseling.

A consultation can be analogous to checking in with Command Central to get your bearings on your earthly travels: "OK, so, right now I'm coming up to the intersection of Maple and Elm Streets. What if I sail on down Elm? Or should I turn right onto Maple? What if I explore that intriguing alleyway, just past Main Street? And over there, it looks like an interesting fruit stand along the road just before that big detour . . ."

And sometimes, we need to call roadside service: "Help! I'm driving into a fog! Where am I going? I can't drive a stick shift." At these times, it is important to be sure that you have called a responsible dispatcher.

Clients who utilize their own multi-sensory gifts become extremely effective conduits themselves. They experience an increase in the accuracy of intuitive hits and find themselves communicating, unmistakably, with loved ones who exist beyond death. They also find themselves perceiving beyond time as easily as they can focus on the present. They become comfortable embracing multi-dimensional perceptions and information that their linear minds cannot translate.

Many of these clients are those whom I invite into my apprenticeship program. I find that my apprentices are dispelling myths about being psychic. Starting out as pretty savvy clients, then apprentices, many progress into full-fledged seers in their own right. They prove that we all have the potential to bring forth and perfect these gifts, given the commitment, some guidance and lots of practice.

You are here to make use of your own personal ability to transmit and receive through your personal, internal broadband connection. I support you in moving into the unknown, free from fear. You are here to become a very powerful being of the future.

How To Go There

Earlier, I referred to Dr. Larry Dossey's description of the non-local mind. Not only are there medical benefits from detaching from a linear perception of time, but doing so will also increase your ability to receive multi-sensory information.

In the biofeedback studies that Dossey reported (page 61), it was found that "paranormal or extrasensory events regularly become more frequent; precognitive dreams may occur; intuition and creativity may flower" after retraining patients' sense of time.

Let your emerging extrasensory abilities assist you in developing a new relationship with the future. It will happen as you suspend your skepticism and become increasingly familiar with new sensations, such as experiencing an occasional glimpse of the future. These "sneak previews" add to your understanding of what is occurring during a particular moment. You receive a clear sense of how a current action, event or thought relates to the future and to the bigger picture. It is a very satisfying, confirming feeling.

When you experience this gift, it adds meaning to situations that you might otherwise consider to be mundane. Your enjoyment in performing daily, routine responsibilities increases. Each task becomes a meditation when you are fully present and in this awareness.

I have mentioned how being present clears your channels to receive intuitive insights. When you slow yourself down and live in the present moment, there is a greater chance of activating the multi-sensory capabilities that will give you the sneak previews of the future. You will experience a shift in your relationship to the future and an awareness best described as a blending of the present *with* the future. By contrast, obsessive speculation about the future takes you away from the portal of the present.

Science fiction novels and movies such as *Bladerunner* often portray futuristic storylines with ominous scenes: . . . rain soaked streets . . . steam escaping from manhole covers . . . dark days. Once, a sudden realization shifted my distant, futuristic visions and integrated them into my present reality. I became conscious of the way those images influenced my perception of future times.

I was driving through Berkeley, California, listening to a talk radio station. The discussion was about carjacking. A policeman was available on the air to chat with listeners who called in. One listener reported that just the day before, while driving along San Pablo Avenue, a gang of young men approached his car as he stopped at a red light. The caller boasted to the policeman, "I showed *them*." He said that he opened his sunroof and tossed out his keys, way out of reach of the perpetrators.

"That's real clever," replied the cop. "They might just as well have shot you." I heard his remark just as I crossed San Pablo Avenue. It happened right here, in my present reality, I thought to myself. I remembered hearing predictions several years before that in years to come there would be this crime called "carjacking."

My futuristic impression of this crime had been ominous, dark and foreboding, like something out of *Road Warrior*. Once I was able to identify where a variation of that occurrence already existed in my present, the fearful images of the future were neutralized.

My point is not to minimize the danger of such violent acts, but rather to show how the texture of the unknown can change with a shift in how you envision the future. Anchoring fears in reality makes them tangible. The bogeyman can snatch you out of the night, but the worst your boss can do is fire you.

I played with my ability to see the future differently. I noticed that when I did so, it no longer loomed over me like a dark cloud. Instantly, I was re-connected to the Source, feeling protected and watched over. I was separate from nothing. Therefore, no one and no thing could harm me. Fears need not separate me from that infinite power.

When I lived in New York City, I noticed that more than one of my friends was afraid to come visit me. Their heads were filled with violent images from too many movies and television shows. Once they took the opportunity to merge negative impressions with reality, their perceptions changed dramatically. When New York City became a known entity, grounded in their own personal reality, they thoroughly enjoyed their visit.

One morning, during a very trying time as a recently divorced mother, I really hit bottom, emotionally. I was in a downward spiral, overwhelmed by my children's needs and financial responsibilities. I felt powerless and ineffective as a mother. The future seemed dark and hopeless. I felt so alone, as though there were no place to turn. I was overcome with an age-old belief: *I must have done something terrible, for God to be punishing me like this.* In desperation, I surrendered to the Source, pleading, "Please help me!"

Suddenly, I felt myself hugged by the warmest blanket of unconditional love. There are no words to describe this embracing sensation. In the next moment, I was illuminated with a crystal clear, profound epiphany: *I was* not *being punished. God must have known that there was something deep within me that I had yet to discover in myself. Otherwise, I would not have been assigned these two children, and under these circumstances.*

With that sudden, intuitive realization, I was instantly transported from a feeling of dark despair to one of exaltation. I felt deeply honored to have been credited with enough love and wisdom to raise those precious souls. The Source must have considered my potential to lead them, love them, honor and protect them. My whole life looked different. I started to spiral back upward.

Foreboding fear dissolves in the present moment when you broaden your view. Similarly, you can see a past and present moment from a new perspective. This can alter your future. It is through the present moment that your future emerges.

We tend to view our life's path as a one-way road, a line that stretches out from point A to point B to C to D and into later time periods. Eventually, the line leads us to our inevitable death, where many fear that they will fall into a dark abyss. Here is one of my favorite "sound bites" that I composed for my book tour in 2000: "*In times ahead, we're going to look back on our perceptions of death the way we now look back on those who thought that the earth was flat and that you could fall off the edge.*"

Desperately, we squint our eyes to see down the road to point G, even though that vista might not be revealed until we reach point E or F. Sometimes point E will pull in events that will have a repositioning effect, thereby allowing us to *recognize* point G.

I know a woman who moved from a very nice apartment to another one with which she became increasingly dissatisfied. "*Why* did I *ever* move here," she lamented. "This one is so much smaller and dingier. *Why* can't I live in an apartment like the one I can see across the way, through my kitchen window?"

The apartment that she gazed longingly upon was precisely the one into which she eventually did move. She had to arrive at point F (the undesirable apartment) before point G (the preferred one) was revealed. Point F had a repositioning effect on her journey. In terms of a linear path, this could be viewed as a natural stop along the route.

In terms of a non-linear, grander scheme emerging, the Universe delivers cues at specific junctures. It does so through synchronistic signals and events that are sent from beyond time and space. It is rare these days to hear an awakening soul respond to an amazing turn of events with, "What a coincidence!"

So, if the woman *had* been able to catch a glimpse of her future apartment, (looking directly from point A to point G) she would have been limited in her ability to interpret what she would see. She might have interpreted it as a residence belonging to someone else, or simply not a possible option. Again, we are only able to interpret through the filter of the present moment. It is a good idea to live with a feeling of expectancy, but without specific expectations.

Moreover, the woman's resulting move to the ideal apartment might not have been her preference at another time. It was not until it came into view through her kitchen window, at point F, that she could appreciate it.

Many strategic components must configure on our paths before the right timing can occur. These components are less dependent upon specific timing than they are relative to the players and events necessary to come together. All the elements are configured and set in motion from beyond time.

One evening while still living in New York, I was walking home from seeing the movie *Sliding Doors*. It was a good depiction of parallel realities. The storyline followed the results that one event had in the life of a young woman who was living in London. In one reality, she caught the Underground (subway) in time to go home to her boyfriend. In the other reality, she missed the train and went on to experience a very different— but parallel—progression of circumstances.

The movie took the viewer through both routes that the woman experienced, simultaneously. The outcome of both paths brought her to pretty much the same juncture, or outcome.

I was thinking about the concept of parallel realities when I reached my residence. There I met up with Ed, an older man who lived in the same building. He was rumored to have been a scientist who worked on the hydrogen bomb. He kept to himself and was always quite secretive about his past, but we often chatted about physics meeting metaphysics. As it turned out, he had also seen *Sliding Doors*.

Ed told me about a psychic reading that he had attended, years before. He said that the psychic described "pieces of colored paper" draped around his shoulders. At the time, she interpreted this to mean that Ed would eventually be traveling to Hawaii. The colored paper must have represented a flowered lei.

Ed said that a few months later he was crossing a street near Sixth Avenue. A building was being torn down further up the street. As he continued walking, a string of colored paper floated down through the air and landing squarely on his shoulders.

"Can you believe the synchronization of time and place that had to come together for that to occur?" Ed mused, scratching his head.

I supposed that this must have seemed phenomenal to Ed the Scientist, who had probably calculated probabilities and linear equations in his head to explain this "coincidence."

"Not at all," I replied. I described to him how I perceived all the elements of that event were configured from beyond time and space. They simply appeared in this dimension and came together at a certain point in time. To perceive such possibilities in a linear way *would* be baffling.

I believe it is in this way that strategic and synchronistic events configure to cross our paths. When you think about your dreams and desires, try to do so without attaching a limiting, linear belief. For example, if you want to move into a fulfilling career, ahead at point D in your life, drop this notion: "I will need to experience a number of prerequisite events and make the logical contacts to get myself from points A to B to C."

When you release such beliefs, your expansive all-knowing, all-seeing Higher Self is free to guide you through unexpected, logic-defying circumstances. By traveling an entirely different route from the one that you had been conditioned to expect, you might attract a job with more depth and enrichment than you could have ever dreamed. But you must stop calculating what your future ought to be. And be prepared for magic.

Once I met a man on a blind date. In the preliminary stages of getting to know each other, he blurted out, "I pretty much figure that in the last ten years of my life, I'm going to have tubes coming out of me. You know, on life support."

I gasped. His conviction about the future shocked me. It felt like the sound of fingernails on a blackboard. "Why in the world are you choosing that future?" I asked.

"Why not?" he replied. "It's just logical. That's what happens when you get old."

Consider how people cheat themselves when they anticipate their journey with fixed perceptions. You might believe that leisure time or relaxation—doing what you really want to do—will enter into your life around point G, during a retirement period. There are infinite ways that these desires can manifest, even back at point A or B. But if you are looking away to point G, you will miss important guidance that will lead you through those possibilities.

You will arrive at the destinations on your path in a much more flowing and enlightened manner as long as you stop trying to manipulate the path to the future. Point A bears its own gifts. Infinite roads lead to unlimited variations of point G. One way or another, you are going to get there. Just put down the map, get onto the bus and hold on to your hat.

Strong Future Events and Free Will

There was a time when I was enjoying frequent discussions with a physical chemist. We were tossing around the question, "How far off your path can your free will take you?" I conjectured that if you let Divine guidance pull you along life's path, you could not stray far. If you exert enough energy and free will, however, you might succeed in opening a few closed doors. But it would be a struggle.

My scientific friend felt that some choices might lead you away from critical destinations. However, you will eventually come to a node, something like those in train switching yards, directing you back toward your destiny. The node might be a seemingly insignificant event, such as sitting next to a stranger on a bus. He is looking to rent out his apartment, one that turns out to be the ideal place that you have been looking for. You end up living two doors from your next girlfriend/boyfriend . . . and so on. Synchronistic events switch you back onto your path.

My friend also expressed some interesting ideas about what he termed "Strong Future Events." We referred to them as "SFEs." They are not necessarily the traditional significant life events, such as graduations, birthdays and funerals. They can be seemingly fickle, fleeting moments, when you could have made one choice, but instead, made another. You could have gone to the right, but you went to the left.

He explained that these SFEs are prevailing future probabilities. I find that they create a strong pull through corridors from a specific moment or event to the present. I make this information practical when I work with clients whose paths seem to present continuous struggles. It often looks as though they are being pulled through a tunnel sideways, staring at the wall, stymied and confused.

In consultations with clients, I often see certain inevitabilities lurking on the horizon. They appear to be in place for the purpose of forcing the surrender of my clients' free will. One client was extremely frustrated that her life was not following her specific agenda. "You are trying to play God," I said. She replied, "Somebody has to!" She was serious.

Life works out best when frustration leads to the release of personal agendas to the grander scheme. When effective, a serendipitous chain of events ensues and ultimately positions these clients to move forward. Their lives start to flow with greater clarity.

Meg is a client who insisted upon exerting her free will. She did everything in her power to become a partner in her law firm. She was so focused on this goal, determined to make it happen, that she was willing to do anything. Maneuvering in ways that compromised her relationships with co-workers, she was eventually fired. A few weeks later, an old friend from law school invited her to lunch. At the last minute, she accepted the invitation.

The two had been very supportive of each other through school and had worked well together on community service projects. Her friend had recently quit an unrewarding government job. They commiserated about their mutual dissatisfaction with the legal profession and joked about the possibility of becoming partners in their own practice. They now work together building a legal practice that is gratifying for both.

When you climb up the wrong way on an escalator, the stairs work against you. Likewise, Strong Future Events can appear to pull you backwards, kicking and screaming. SFEs often pull us through toxic patterns that are counter-productive to the soul's evolution. They are revealed by the exaggeration or repetition of those themes. The challenge is to surrender to new perceptions about your life and experience the resulting shift in reality. As a result, you are likely to find yourself strategically repositioned, facing the right direction on the escalator.

One always has the option to set aside egocentric desires and defer to the bigger plan: "Let Thy will—not mine—be done." Give in to what God is telling you through the events in your life. The Universe will then be able to deliver joy and new adventures because you are no longer resisting.

One of my favorite concepts is what I call "perverted joy." This is when people live their whole lives so as to prove victim beliefs about themselves. In the end, on their deathbeds, they proclaim with a strong sense of righteousness, "See? I was right! Nothing ever went my way!" These unfortunate souls, so focused on being right, never realized that they were walking the wrong way up the escalator. No wonder they never got anywhere.

A certain kind of SFE can have harsh and lasting impact. A seemingly innocent, fleeting or insignificant decision can result in tremendous grief or misfortune. Jobs can be jeopardized, relationships can be ruined and lives can be lost. People may lament endlessly that they did not made a different choice. Sometimes, however, it was not their choice to make.

Nan is a client who left the cap off the kerosene can in her garage. She will forever live in torment over the loss of her two-year-old son who drank the solution while he played. He was unsupervised for only a few short moments.

In California, a father forgot his infant son in the back seat of his car while he went into work on a sweltering day. He will replay that fatal morning the rest of his life, wondering at what juncture he might have made a different choice and spared his son's life.

Employees who made the fatal choice to return to their desks in the World Trade Center left their loved ones forever re-running "what if . . ." scenarios.

Seemingly fickle wrong turns that lead to such tragedies might actually be SFEs that are configured to draw those exact circumstances onto one's path. From a larger perspective, experiencing the unimaginable might be a soul requirement for growth. Disasters and loss offer opportunities for expansion and evolution. They catalyze spiritual awakening and balance karmic scenarios.

It is not uncommon for me to communicate with souls on the Other Side who confirm that their exit route was no accident. They often indicate that they are currently very involved in work to be done in the non-physical dimension. In many cases, those projects position them for subsequent re-entries. They share glimpses of those paths ahead.

When the path of the willing participant—the "victim"— is one of a child, it may be a configuration that is designed to bestow that soul with wisdom gained from experiencing the part it played. Then the soul is released to return "home." An

133

exit may also be timed so that the soul can re-enter to execute a subsequent, specific mission in the physical dimension.

That re-entry might coincide with a key placement in history. Perhaps it will involve a more opportune time for the evolution of that soul. Or that re-entry might enable the soul to team up with a group of souls for a collective purpose.

I once did a Reading in the Round for a group who all lived on the same street, in a cul-de-sac. Tiffany was a young mother of two who had also lived there but had died from influenza a few months before. She communicated messages to each one in the group as I went around the circle.

It became apparent that the entire group had been guided to live in that particular neighborhood for a unified purpose: to awaken spiritually and realign with the Source. I discovered that as pioneers, living in another life space, this soul-group had died of starvation and exposure. They cursed God for their misfortune.

Figuratively, this group had once again circled the wagons: this time, in the cul-de-sac. Their awakening was triggered by the loss of their beloved friend. Now this group meditates together and cultivates a neighborhood garden.

I also recall Olivia, who called me with an urgent concern. Her son, Jeremy, had been killed. His body was found lying on railroad tracks near a beach, unrecognizable. I told her that I do not usually consult for cases involving mayhem, except where that type of information enters into the landscape of a bigger picture. I referred her to a psychic who worked with the police and FBI. She decided to call upon us both.

At the beginning of her phone consultation, Jeremy projected himself to me clearly, exclaiming, "The experiment worked!" He related, telepathically, that from his life review process, he now understood that the way he passed was influenced by karmic circumstances. He confirmed to Olivia that she had indeed been in communication with him the night of his death. He was also aware that his passing had been the catalyst for the spiritual awakening of his father and sister.

"I know that Dad is grieving terribly," Jeremy said, "but please tell him to stay focused. He could hit his hand with a hammer next week." Olivia said that her husband worked as a building contractor.

Then Jeremy listed the names of several of his friends who had surfed with him at the beach that day. "I know they are in pain. They blame themselves for leaving me to walk home that day, along the railroad tracks," he acknowledged. "Please tell them that there is no way they should have done anything differently."

Jeremy turned to me, asking me (telepathically) to explain my version of SFEs to his mother. Just as I was able to access his consciousness, he could do the same with mine. He had picked up on my reference to SFEs. I explained the inevitability of Strong Future Events to Olivia.

I am not advocating that we should not always try to do the right thing and contribute whatever we can for one another. But most SFEs are impossible to override. In Jeremy's case, his friends played a crucial part in his life's journey, but they were not responsible for the outcome of the event.

Olivia had another consultation several months later. She asked if I would consider looking into any details about Jeremy's death. The police had uncovered very little and the psychic to whom I had referred her had not been able to help. She knew my hesitation. I did agree to see what might be revealed in a larger context, rather than to explore grizzly details. At the onset of this session, Jeremy arrived to describe the karmic significance of his death.

I moved into Jeremy's consciousness at the time of his passing and saw through his eyes. Three men were standing before him. One with a tattoo on his arm, one with a knife. The third looked into Jeremy's eyes. Jeremy looked right back, almost through this man, the moment the knife was thrust into him. I told Olivia that I felt that this man was ready to confess.

Then Jeremy showed me a scene from a past life space. He was a warrior, stalking his foe in grassy marshlands, cutting his way through very tall reeds. He came face to face with three of the enemy whom he was ordered to kill.

For a brief moment he hesitated, looking into the eyes of one of his adversaries. He paused, indecisive as to whether to kill his adversaries with his sword—as commanded—or to follow his heart and spare their lives. He shook away his hesitation and proceeded to kill them. Apparently Jeremy's death was a re-enactment of a past scenario with one or more of the same cast of characters. This time, Jeremy played the victim. A deep karmic connection was formed, then confirmed, when the two looked into each other's souls at the moment of their physical deaths.

Olivia said that when Jeremy was in high school, he wrote a composition about a soldier who faced three men he was ordered to kill. He wrote about the dilemma, whether to follow through or set them free. I said, "It seems that he was writing from a soul memory."

The most baffling, nonsensical relationships and events that come in and out of all our lives are often those that run the deepest in terms of karma seeking balance. Generally, when you are spiritually awakened, you are an unlikely candidate for such karmic vignettes.

When you are alert, present and awakened, you are able to gain insights from the themes and lessons as they present themselves.

You learn vicariously from observing the way that challenges unfold and are resolved in others' lives. You create less need to act out dramatic events. Closure and balance result from the insights rather than necessitating the arduous experience of a karmic lesson. I call it "jumping off the karmic conveyor belt."

Our fears and misperceptions derail us. They can turn us away from the beam of Divine energy. However, our timeless journey can be balanced. The enlightening insights promote shifts in perception, which gets us back on track. The resulting effect places us back in the "beam" to receive the ultimate gift of Grace. Love flows through, unconditionally.

One client, living in Big Bear, California, experienced an SFE that pulled her in a positive way. One day, she and her husband were shopping in San Bernardino, the town at the foot of Big Bear Mountain. Late in the afternoon, they contemplated driving on to Palm Springs for dinner. At the last moment, they decided to drive home, back up the mountain.

A few moments after they arrived in the driveway, they found themselves standing in the front doorway (as Californians are taught to do) with their arms around their teenage daughter. It was the exact moment of a major earthquake. If they had chosen to dine in Palm Springs, their daughter might have experienced the quake frightened and alone. Most likely, their decision had not been their choice to make.

I have a delightful recollection of a time when everything in my life configured as the result of the magnetizing pull from an SFE. I have to say that by now it is becoming easier for me to identify this phenomenon even as it starts to gain momentum in my present, rather than becoming identifiable to me only in retrospect.

I was traveling around the U.S. on an extensive book tour, waiting in long lines in too many airports. Hotels and other accommodations made quick-energy, unhealthy food too readily available to me. When I am tired and overworked, there is a ravenous "cookie monster" in me that grabs up any delectable morsels within reach. He tosses them my way for my immediate, gluttonous consumption. Usual prey for this monster can appear in the form of the complimentary cookies, such as those typically found at a Seattle B&B. The cookie monster went wild on that particular tour.

I returned to New York, tired, undernourished and plumped up. I can usually resume my healthier eating routine right away, once I am home. Normally, I reduce my travel weight back to a more attractive, comfortable range within a couple of days. But the cumulative result of this trip's eating left my weight residing on the near side of porky. Something compelled me to set up an altogether different routine. All the doors opened and pulled me into a perfect, unanticipated regimen.

Shortly after my return, I happened to stop in at the Integral Yoga Center, just down the street from where I lived. Not only were there classes available that jibed with my schedule, but there was also an opening for a volunteer to work in the kitchen at noontime. I could exchange work hours for free classes and lunches with the staff. This appealed to me, offering me a new way to get acquainted with new people and share a meal with enlightening folks. I had found it challenging to meet people in New York while running my own, very solitary business. Barhopping had never been my cup of tea.

Three times a week, I washed community-sized pots and pans with a dancer from Brazil, an actor from Julliard and a nearly homeless divorcee. I ate wonderful organic lunches with yoga teachers and stimulating residents from the Yoga Community. Between the beginning of November and the end of January, I effortlessly dropped the excess tonnage I had accumulated on the road.

In December I was invited to speak on my first cruise, due to embark that following February. I would never have anticipated the need to be in my best shape for a winter event. I believe that the cruise was a SFE and it created a magnetic pull from that future to the present, just as I was retuning home. It brought about a synchronization of events that primed me to arrive on board in good shape.

The Continuum of Consciousness

I enjoy receiving endless examples that our soul is truly eternal. It carries with it aspects of all that we have ever been and all that we have experienced, through a continuous stream of consciousness.

In *Heart-Links* I relate the example of a client who, in a future moment, was watching her yet unborn little boy walking towards her. In that future moment she was aware that there existed a connection between this soul and a good friend of hers in the past. A few months before the consultation, a close friend of hers passed from a terminal illness. Before passing, she said to my client, "I really like the man you married. He would make a great father. Hey, I ought to come back as your child." And indeed, that had come about.

In London, I was consulting for a very successful entrepreneur who had practiced meditation for years. He was not surprised when his wife joined us to confirm that she was doing well since her passing from cancer. My client felt that he was in touch with her on an ongoing basis. His wife began our three-way chat, opening with, "About that final conversation we were having before we were so rudely interrupted by my death . . . " This was a superb demonstration of the seamless continuum of consciousness.

I did a phone consultation for Paige, a repeating client who has lived most of her life in Southern California. In 1989 she attended a drama program in England at the British American Drama Academy at Oxford University. There she met and fell in love with a young man named John. He was fifteen years old at the time, and she was twenty-one. John had been attending high school in Maryland before they met in England.

John aspired to be a dancer. He and Paige had a mutual friend at the Academy who was six foot four to John's five foot eight. One day when they were all standing outside chatting together, John looked over at Paige and smiled. Then he walked about ten feet away, took a running start and did a split leap over their friend's head. He walked back over to Paige and said with a grin, "It's the closest thing to flying."

At the time, Paige was discovering that she was an "empath," intuitively feeling what others feel, and was exploring the extent of her intuitive abilities. John expressed that he wanted to learn from her. They had long discussions about philosophy.

From the time that Paige and John first met, they felt a connection. They discussed reincarnation, and John said how "cool" it would be to return one day as Paige's child. Paige didn't pay much attention.

Apparently, John's sister had taken her own life a few years before. Paige mentioned to John that he could never know how his sister might turn up again in his life one day. When she suggested that she could even reincarnate as a child of his own, John turned to Paige and said, very seriously, "No, I think that I will come back as *your* child!" This time, she understood that he meant it. Considering his age, she laughed. Then she replied, "Now *that* would be difficult."

The age difference was challenging for Paige, which she did not hesitate to express to John before they left England. John, on the other hand, had no problem being with an older woman. John spent the next three years back in Maryland. The physical distance between them further prevented any chance for a relationship.

Later, John invited Paige to visit him at UC Berkeley, where he had decided to attend college. She declined. He did, however, come down to visit her in Los Angeles. Even though Paige was dating someone else at the time, she and John found that they were still in love.

After that, Paige traveled up to San Francisco on business and did take the time to meet with John. This time, John had found someone new, but again, their meeting confirmed their love for each other. It was shortly after that last meeting that Paige learned that John had been shot and killed by a mugger in Berkeley.

John passed when he was twenty years old, two months after his birthday in 1993. He started visiting Paige in her dreams almost immediately after his murder. She said, "It wasn't long afterwards that I was talking to him 'in my head.'" Later, she understood that these were very real conversations and that he has been looking out for her for quite some time.

At the time of Paige's most recent consultation, she reminded me that in a reading two years earlier, I had interpreted for John from the Other Side. He still maintained that he would eventually return as Paige's child. "Your job," he told her, "will be to keep me focused on my spiritual path." I confirmed that when John was killed, he ejected from his body "like being shot out of a canon." Then John said, "Now I can *really* fly!"

John pantomimed someone using a pair of scissors. Paige was dating a man who had a vasectomy. This is how he got me to ask Paige how he might return to her if her boyfriend could not "contribute" to the project.

At the end of Paige's consultation, she told me that she was no longer dating that man and that she had applied to adopt a baby. She had no idea when this would come about. In that reading, John said that it would be "soon," that the birth mother would be from California and that there would be a "synchronicity with the timing."

John also said he would be returning as a daughter because that is what Paige would prefer, since she was going to be a single mom. He said that her spiritual awareness would serve as the "tarmac for his flight" as a metaphysician in this life.

John said that as Paige's daughter, he will be certain to remind her frequently that they are only pretending that he is the younger one. He plans to demonstrate this to her by doing things before she shows him how. The two examples he gave in the consultation involved riding a tricycle and being able to hold a fork or a spoon.

Paige now believes that John was having a premonition when he expressed his desire to return as her child one day. She said, "When he first made that statement, the look in his eyes told me he was stating a fact. From that moment, we talked about it as if it were a certainty. I can't even tell you why. I was the only one of the two of us who prefaced the statements with, 'If you should leave this life before I do . . . ' John never did. He would simply say, 'When I come back as your child . . . '"

Paige told me that the mere fact that she was able to get a consultation with me the last time I was in Southern California was, in itself, serendipitous. She said, "I was lying in bed very late one night and started thinking that I should find out when you would be in L.A. It became so important that I got up to search for my old tape that very night ... after midnight. I couldn't sleep until I found it. Then I accessed your website. It turned out that you were in the area that very same weekend. You just 'happened' to have a cancellation. John wanted to tell me he was on the way."

CJ is another soul who transmitted through timeless consciousness from a "no-time zone" before birth. He presented a fascinating "sneak preview" of events that would occur after his birth. At the time of this consultation, Kerri, his mother, was eighteen weeks pregnant. The baby's mother confirmed much of this information when her son was two months old.

CJ began by alerting Kerri to the fact that he would reenter carrying an aspect of "Harry." Kerri said that Harry was the grandfather whom she never met. He passed before her birth.

CJ also said that throughout his childhood he would be very attracted to "the one who jingles keys or coins." Kerri said that this is a well-known characteristic of her father-in-law, who rattles his keys constantly. In a recent communication she wrote, "CJ has already successfully turned this rough and tough, seventy-year-old Ph.D. businessman into mush."

Among several "sneak previews" that CJ projected were the images of a dog hitting its head, a mobile looking to be off-balance and something about an ice cream truck driving by. His mother reported that these three events transpired in the same day.

First, she noticed that the baby seemed a bit agitated while lying in his crib. She straightened his tilted mobile. A little later in the day, the dog sneezed so hard that he hit his head on the floor. She said that CJ laughed, almost uncontrollably. (More than one soul has cautioned a mother-to-be, projecting

" . . . and when you see me laugh after I'm born, know that it is not gas!") About the same time that day, she heard the song from the ice cream truck going down their street.

Before writing this account, I confirmed these details with CJ's mother. She sent me some fun information that further shows the challenge of trying to interpret the future in terms of the present. She wrote:

"In my first consultation you were conversing with my grandmother who had passed. She was telling you something about a bird flittering in the corner of a house. It appeared to you that that the bird had become trapped. I believed this was a time when I saw a bird overhead and felt certain that it was my grandmother's presence.

"However, while typing this just now, sitting out in my backyard, my husband approached me. He was holding a folded towel in his hands. He said, 'Hey! Do you want to see a magic trick?' He opened the towel and out flew a bird! I couldn't stop laughing.

"Then the bird flew to perch on the fence. I watched him and he sat there for a few minutes, looking back at me. I think that my grandmother was alerting us to a future moment, this one that just now happened in the present. She must have known that I would be in contact with you, right at this time."

These souls, transmitting before birth, are wonderful examples of the continuum of consciousness that we will be witnessing in times ahead. More and more souls will reincarnate, remembering. And their parents will not be discounting their children's intuitive sensing or the "memories" they recall.

The mothers of both of these souls were invited into my apprenticeship program after I assessed the level of their own multi-sensory abilities. They demonstrated trust in multi-dimensional awareness, even when their rational minds discount what is being received. In the apprenticeship program, I have no hesitation in sharing all my "secrets" and tools in an effort to further the next wave of extremely aware and "dialed" individuals. They are the bridge to the future.

Interpreting the Future

Earlier, I summarized an interesting investigation by Peter Russell regarding a probable future shift in consciousness. His influence underlined a compelling new emphasis for my work. This emphasis is a determination to assist others in aligning themselves with their true and eternal spirit. I am resolved to empower people with a realization of their true identity. I seek to facilitate the repositioning of people to face forward and open up to an entirely new existence.

Glimpses of the future can only be interpreted in terms of the present. And present perceptions are unavoidably influenced by experiences from the past. For this reason, I take great pains in consultations to interpret future information every possible way—literally, symbolically and metaphorically. I encourage clients to receive all that their linear, "local" minds cannot comprehend. It is only through passage of time that the most accurate interpretation of the future unfolds. Time will tell.

I ask clients to keep the future images I interpret during consultations "lightly on the shelf." I instruct them to resist the urge to obsess about identifying what has been prognosticated.

The tendency is to impose their desired interpretation onto subsequent events. To do so is a sure way to pull out of the present and miss important guidance—and the access to that future. In any event, speculation about the future is less engaging the more you live in the present and without fear.

I personally had a dramatic example of the challenge in accurately interpreting the future. Years ago, when my daughter was twelve years old, she came into my bedroom where I was meditating. She sat on the bed and sighed, "Mom, I just don't think that I'm ever going to get married." Being in a relaxed and somewhat transcendent state, I unexpectedly saw a vision around her. There was the letter "J," and that person wore white.

At the time, I was raising my daughter in Newport Beach, California. I could only interpret this image in terms of my present repertoire of experiences. Naturally, I deciphered this to mean that she might eventually meet a "Jim" or a "John"—quite possibly a tennis player, a doctor or a dentist.

How incredulous I would have been had my future self tapped me on the shoulder at that moment and whispered into my ear: "Excuse me, Louise ... but, uh, what you are seeing there, is that your daughter will eventually convert to Judaism and meet a man over a particular holiday when he is wearing white.

"His name will be Joseph. She will marry him and join the strictest Hasidic tribe in Jerusalem, where she will live more happily than ever in her life. In that foreign land, the two of them will raise your grandchildren who will speak only Yiddish!"

This was years before I relocated to New York City. I could not have entertained the faintest idea of the meaning of

"Hasidic." The other elements of that eventual reality would have been equally incomprehensible to me. How futile it would have been to interpret that future with the limited perspective available to me in that present.

I believe in a future, an existence that will truly reflect the nature of our eternal, divinely generated spirit. Given the prospects of an eventual shift in consciousness, it is a reality in which our natural multi-sensory abilities will be fully operative. Multidimensional understanding will no longer be funneled through limited linear perceptions.

Fear is a product of the dual nature of this physical dimension. Duality offers us the opportunity to experience the dark and the Light. The darkness serves as a contrasting backdrop that makes the Light more discernable. Inarguably, our world is becoming pretty dark. As the Light gets brighter, it casts a wider shadow. The more distinct the Light becomes, the more effective a beacon it becomes to lead us out of the darkness.

In the future, such conceptions of duality will fall away. We will experience life without duality, without the need to learn from contrasting experiences. We will expand without the need to define ourselves by comparing "that which I am, by that which I am not."

The soul recognizes truth. With the increasing illumination in this world projected against the backdrop of a darkening landscape, people will not tolerate that which is not spoken in truth. Nor will they support decisions that originate from inauthentic motives.

Given the limitations of interpreting the future in the context of the present, I will share a future to which I was once transported, in a spontaneous, unexpected, single moment that transcended this dimension. Years ago, I was driving down the "Grapevine," a long stretch of highway that extends from Bakersfield, California, over the mountains and into Los Angeles.

As I was driving, an overwhelming feeling of gratitude swept over me. This was accompanied by a sense of tremendous awe for the infinite workings of the Universe. Suddenly, I shifted to expanded consciousness while continuing to safely drive my car.

I experienced an amazing future that I assumed to exist in another dimension. I could not tell if I was an occupant in this living community or a visitor from the past. Rather than appearing as a New-Age-ish commune, it was more a coming together of very present, grounded souls.

Incidentally, I get impatient with those who feel that they ought to become more "cosmic" or "airy-fairy" in order to be more intuitive and multi-dimensional. I always caution, "Be here, now. You must ground the wire to be an effective receiver." After a talk at a bookstore, a woman once approached me to ask, "Can you tell that I am one who always seems to get things in series of threes?" I replied, "No, no, no."

For some to contemplate the idea of people living in a community is to conjure up images from the 1960s: flower children walking around in gauze clothing, high on mind-altering substances and free love. Members of those communities often served a patriarchal guru. Often, the emphasis on the community's goals compromised the individual's sense of wellbeing or integrity.

In this future, I observed people living with greater dignity than in the stereotypical communal experience. Many ran their own small businesses, similar to a growing trend today. Some worked in an elaborate communication network that connected this particular community to many others around the world. The technology that supports greater autonomy in our current age of communication and links people to each other had developed in unimaginable ways.

Most people who lived in this community were involved in some form of creative arts. They felt inspired to express themselves from the heart. It has been said: "Creativity is Divine energy expressing itself."

In my current life space, I am already seeing traces of new creative avenues that I cannot define in today's terms. For example, I once described a moment that existed in the future of an artist client. She was able to bring sound through color. She said that she was having dreams where she saw people standing and looking at her painting, hearing celestial choirs.

In the future community, I saw children learning expressive dance and movement. Young people were painting very large murals that coordinated beautifully with the architecture of nearby buildings. Those buildings blended unobtrusively with the lush, natural landscape that surrounded them.

The verdant vegetation looked greener than I had ever seen. Beautiful gardens, which were created without genetic manipulation, grew without pesticides. There were new hybrids of plants that thrived in soil composed of new elements. The population had a reverent respect for all that nature provided, cultivating no more than what was needed to sustain the community.

I remember the brilliant red of tomatoes in one of the vegetable gardens that caught my attention. There were outdoor garden plots and indoor greenhouses. Flowers bordered the community in decorative gardens. They also grew in large fields in a nearby valley. The land looked fertile with dark rich soil covering the natural inclines and slopes. The community clustered around the natural formation of two or three lakes and streams.

At one point, I found myself participating in some sort of ceremony. Participants were standing in a circle on a hill. The purpose seemed to be in preparation for a gathering to take place within the next couple of days. A boat was bringing a delegation of emissaries from another community. Both communities were guided by spiritual priorities that served the greater good. Standing with these people, I felt new sensations that I have never experienced.

I was instantly aware of the telepathic communication that linked us all. The moment that I joined with the others in the circle, I became aware of their thoughts and sensed that they knew mine. When feelings of love and gratitude swept over me they looked my way, smiled and nodded. They had a way of acknowledging intuitively who I was, as if they had always known me on a very deep level.

Telepathy was used as an efficient and complete method of communication. By contrast, written and spoken communication seemed laborious and contrived. Subtle nuances and intentions were instantly conveyed telepathically, adding depth and flavor to communication. So much could be transmitted so quickly, beyond words. It was hard to know who had "spoken" first. It reminded me of how it works when I interpret for loved ones on the Other Side.

Each person was able to access a group mind. This ability prompted creative ideas to grow exponentially from the contribution of many minds envisioning together. At the same time, the group mind allowed for the contribution of each person's unique perspective.

Each individual joined in with a clear and intuitive sense of his or her own role within the community. Diversity was valued and respected. There were no enemies, since there existed no perception of any one being separate from another.

People were not motivated by any desire to rival each other. All maintained and lived by a unified vision. Man had finally learned that there truly is enough love to go around.

In physics, entrainment is the effect of one frequency joining with another oscillating frequency. First there is dissonance, then resonance, as the one frequency starts to vibrate with the other. The new vibration is entrained or brought into resonance with the other. Discordant thoughts could be entrained and brought into harmony. Sound and color were used to heal energy fields that were disturbed or out of balance.

There seemed to be this effect of entrainment when I sensed the group's thoughts combining. Sometimes, in my present reality, I feel a somewhat less unified version of this. When I conduct "Readings in the Round," I tune into a group of ten participants at the same time. It is often a group of individuals who have not previously met each other. Most of them share a mutual intention to receive information that will enlighten and heal. By the end of the evening, they are on the same wavelength, as if they have been friends for a long time.

In the future community, telepathic communication was effortless. I can only guess that it evolved naturally as a result of deep, personal inner healing. Consciousness was unclouded and undistracted by personal issues. It became evident that the outer projections of man's inner chaos were the greatest challenges that had confronted civilization. That realization affected tremendous emotional healing in the world. People's thoughts and consciences were clear. With nothing to hide, telepathy was easy.

In my present work, I enjoy the way telepathic communication transcends any language barriers. Clients often ask how it is that I can interpret for a loved one who spoke a foreign language in their physical life. Their gestures may exaggerate a particular cultural characteristic, but transmission and reception is easy. This type of communication circumvents the limitations of linear, verbal language.

The entire future community would call on a Higher Power for one in need. Some were able to come to others through dreams. Dream interpretation promoted healing and greater understanding of problems or lessons to be learned.

With illumination of personal dark shadows, people no longer obsessed about ways to maneuver, dominate or manipulate others. I experienced an awareness of complete understanding of, and gratitude for, individual talents that contributed quite perfectly to the whole.

The emptiness and frustration that people had come to feel from believing in the illusion of the material world necessitated a worldwide spiritual awakening. Each individual's divine connection was recognized and confirmed—for it has always existed. Motivations were Divinely inspired and guided.

This community was entirely self-sufficient, materially and economically. It was also politically autonomous. Those who served in leadership roles were supported by the group consensus. People were not elected to positions through any political process that I could identify.

The delegation of roles and duties was obvious to the whole, understood through more refined intuitive sensing. The capacity through which each person served the community was one that they performed the most effectively, utilizing individual talents and gifts to the fullest. People contributed their gifts freely. The community thrived and was nurtured by the contribution of these valuable gifts.

When I became aware of personal relationships in this future existence, it was evident that through self-healing, all were quite capable of taking care of themselves. This independence left much more room for adventure. The old obsession for unrealistic romantic expectations no longer existed.

Both male and female energy were recognized and balanced in both sexes. This balance allowed everyone to share and contribute as integrated beings. This supported a personal observation of mine: When men and woman are in a seduction mode, they are often unconsciously trying to reach for the energy of the opposite sex and bring it into themselves.

A "macho" guy might pursue women who embody the feminine aspects of intuition, vulnerability and the ability to nurture. Likewise, a woman who lacks more assertive, proactive, rational aspects might attempt to bring it to herself by being seductive around men who exude that kind of strength.

I saw men and women living in a balanced way in the future. It allowed both sexes to enjoy and support healthier qualities in each other. There was no desperate need to control or take anything from each other.

It was evident to me in this future that children were valued and respected for the wisdom they brought forth at birth. No longer were they treated as lesser beings because of their chronological age. They remembered who they were and from "where" they had come.

I remember the time that I laughed long and hard when a client told me something that her three-year-old granddaughter had said. The little girl looked in the mirror and exclaimed, "Goodness! *I'm a BABY!*"

Children in this future were taught to trust themselves at an early age. Adults took the time to listen and validate their perceptions and feelings. They were also encouraged to talk about their dreams as they learned how to work out personal issues through lucid dreaming.

Intuitive abilities come naturally to children in our world, but they fade with exposure to parental and societal skepticism. In this future, multi-sensory abilities were easily integrated into life experiences.

It was gratifying to see that in this future, the elderly were no longer invisible. They were considered to be vital and valuable members of the community. They were relied upon for their experience and their wisdom.

People became more interesting and interested with every birthday. Even though there did not seem to be physical aging, there was still a sense of certain souls who were valued for carrying greater wisdom, as if from having lived and learned over a longer span of time. Young people once again respected and admired their "elders."

Attitudes and beliefs about aging had changed dramatically. In the way that form follows thought, the physical body's aging process was transformed. With their awakening, people had become attentive to the body's efficient way of communicating its needs and requirements. People listened to their bodies' messages, which alerted them to any issues. It was therefore unnecessary for the body to manifest disease to get its owner's attention.

With no clocks or watches in this future, people moved through their days in accordance with their own natural rhythm, in sync with the light of day and with the seasons. Life was in rhythm with the earth. The seasons were different, although I cannot really describe why, or how this came about.

Without an imposing linear perspective, stress was nonexistent. People worked and played together. Both were equally valued activities. No one worried that he/she would run out of time. There was no need to save it.

I speculate that one effect from current and future weather changes is that survival issues will force people into a more tribal, community-focused way of living. It will certainly influence how people live and care about each other. It is important to notice the indicators that are already leading us in that direction.

Occasionally in the present, I alert clients to future opportunities that will encourage or even impose this kind of awareness. For one client, I described a scene where a fire was likely to start down the street from her home.

The scene was neither ominous nor foreboding. Rather, it indicated an opportunity. Previously, the residents in this neighborhood were living without awareness of each other, isolated behind their satellite dishes and automatic garage doors. The neighbors would be forced to come together, exchange phone numbers and share meals.

Your future awaits you in this very moment.

It is adventurous to the degree that you are willing to leap beyond your comfort zone and embrace the uncertainty of the future. It will guide you on to new journeys.

It is challenging to the degree that you are resistant to learn and grow from life's lessons. The future does not cater to the ego-self.

It is exciting to the degree that you are willing to release your confining expectations to a greater wisdom. It will reveal fantastic insights.

It is meaningful to the degree that you are able to surrender your confusion, seeking guidance and clarity. You are not alone.

It is forgiving to the degree that you are willing to forgive others. Grace is a gift bestowed freely.

It is responsive to all your needs to the degree that you have learned to take care of yourself and ask for what you need. God helps those who help themselves.

It embraces you with unconditional love, to the degree that you are able to love and accept yourself. If you would have love and acceptance in your life, then demonstrate them to the world and your future will reflect both back to you.

It protects you from your enemies to the degree that you no longer see yourself as separate from anyone. In the absence of separation, no one will try to harm you any more than they would try to harm themselves.

It is patient, waiting for you to ask the right questions. It will show you who you are when you ask, "Who am I?"

Step through the portal of the present into the fearless future. You are here to experience it through each passing moment. It is what you came here to do.

Epilogue

*"Reality is merely an illusion,
albeit a very persistent one."*

—Albert Einstein

I recently found myself feeling fearful when I heard some information regarding potential terrorist activity and earth-shift predictions. The information came to me in the same day, from several directions. I must have been attracting it.

Fortunately, this encroaching perspective triggered a reminder: my need to stay out of fear. Fears have such a contracting effect on my whole outlook. Through the week I observed my usual optimism about life's infinite possibilities steadily diminish. Those of potential impending disaster took their place.

Determined to retreat from fear, I forced myself to bring the precepts of this book back to mind and to practice what I preach. I remembered to come back into the present and made myself recall how certain aspects of the future (now in the past) used to look to me at various junctures of my life.

By now, those speculated future moments have passed by in entirely different shapes and sizes. They were outside the scope of my most active imagination. Sometimes they arrived as growth-promoting challenges. But most often, they arrived through synchronistic, creative and adventurous avenues.

I also remembered my advice to the reader, to become at ease with the impermanence of all things. Life is continually in motion and ever changing. I am, myself, a work in progress. When I anticipate future possibilities, I usually forget that for myself, I can only see to Point B.

By the time I arrive at Point B, I will be changed by the experiences that led me there. If I stay awake, I will arrive there more evolved with new perspectives, greater wisdom and life-shifting insights. Point C will take on a whole new interpretation.

Indeed, it is important for me to maintain a "heads-up" awareness. I need to steer clear of the mindless choices made by those who are motivated by fear.

It is also important for me to stay mindful of the increasing vulnerability of certain locations on the planet. I need to remember that I will be guided to all the right locations in all moments. I am resolved to let this awareness flow into a safe place in the periphery of my consciousness.

By taking myself through this process, I found that I came back to center. I stepped back into "the beam" of Divine energy where clear guidance is not elusive. It will not fail to take me where I need to go.

When I am no longer a physical being, I will want to see that I approached every possible adventure with expectancy, but without expectations. I will want to have experienced each and every event consciously and fully . . . and not in fear.

Being Fearless Among the Fearful

Years ago, I signed up for a year of law school. Looking back upon the experience, I would now define it as a totally unremarkable, free-will choice that I made at a directionless time in my life. I achieved so-so grades, I did not meet anyone with whom I stayed in contact, and I found the reading and reporting of legal cases to be a tedious waste of time. I also had to contend with an annoying distraction from deceased plaintiffs and defendants who would contact me during class discussions to telepathically communicate their side of a case.

With each approaching midterm and final, I remember feeling a contagious hysteria that spread like smoke through hallways. It was spawned from a fear of being unprepared. Frantic whispers in the elevators made me nervous: "Get Barons for torts!" or "You'll nail contracts with . . . " Rather than a benevolent gesture to reach out and help others, it seemed to be more an attempt to appear to have the inside scoop on how to cinch exams. Competition for future internships prevented that kind of altruism.

People do strange things when trapped in the contracting emotion of fear. Once you observe yourself in a moment of fear, then try to identify the fear, embrace it (rather than deny or run from it) and shift to a feeling of gratitude—for anything that you can think of at the time. You will immediately find yourself out of fear and back to center, where you can sense more clearly and make more responsible choices.

When you find yourself *among* the fearful, you may need to show others how to rise above the herd and take the high road. When I do this, simply taking that action diverts me from judging others for the ridiculous way they might be acting.

For example, people sometimes cut in front of others in line when they fear being left behind. Show them how to be courteous. This happened to me recently in Israel. I was standing up to get off a bus when a woman shoved ahead of me, nearly knocking me back down into my seat. I stood back up, assuming that her husband, behind her, would then let me go ahead of him. Seeing that he had no intention of making space for me, I smiled and gestured for him to go ahead. The man standing *behind* him had watched all this unfold, then smiled at me and gestured for me to go ahead of him. Kindness was catching on.

You become a more powerful being in any moment that you simply pause ... and allow Divine energy to flow through you. You will be moved to act in ways that demonstrate fearlessness and compassion. This is how you become "a light in the market place."